EXECUTIONS AND HANGINGS IN NEWCASTLE AND MORPETH

FOUL DEEDS AND SUSPICIOUS DEATHS Series

Wharncliffe's *Foul Deeds and Suspicious Deaths* series explores, in detail, crimes of passion, brutal murders and foul misdemeanors from early modern times to the present day. Victorian street crime, mysterious deaths and modern murders tell tales where passion, jealousy and social deprevation brought unexpected violence to those involved. From unexplained death and suicide to murder and manslaughter, the books provide a fascinating insight into the lives of both victims and perpetrators as well as society as a whole.

Other titles in the series

Please contact us via any of the methods below for more information or a catalogue.
WHARNCLIFFE BOOKS
47 Church Street – Barnsley – South Yorkshire – S70 2AS
Tel: 01226 734555 – 734222 Fax: 01226 734438
E-mail: enquiries@pen-and-sword.co.uk – Website: www.wharncliffebooks.co.uk

Executions and Hangings in

NEWCASTLE AND MORPETH

MAUREEN ANDERSON

Series Editor
Brian Elliott

Wharncliffe Books

First Published in Great Britain in 2005 by
Wharncliffe Books
an imprint of
Pen and Sword Books Ltd
47 Church Street
Barnsley
South Yorkshire
S70 2AS

Copyright © Maureen Anderson, 2005

ISBN: 1-903425-91-3

A CIP catalogue record for this book is available from the
British Library.

Typeset in 11/13pt Plantin by Mac Style Ltd, Scarborough.

Printed and bound in England by
CPI UK.

Pen and Sword Books Ltd incorporates the Imprints of
Pen & Sword Aviation, Pen & Sword Maritime,
Pen & Sword Military, Wharncliffe Books,
Pen & Sword Select, Pen and Sword Military Classics
and Leo Cooper.

For a complete list of Pen & Sword titles please contact
PEN & SWORD BOOKS LIMITED
47 Church Street
Barnsley
South Yorkshire
S70 2BR
England
E-mail: enquiries@pen-and-sword.co.uk
Website: www.pen-and-sword.co.uk

Contents

James Berry, assisted by John Morley, carried out the execution of Patrick Judge at Newcastle in 1875. Author's collection

Introduction

There have been many forms of execution in Britain including shooting, burning, beheading, pressing to death (for those who would not plead to a crime) and hanging. Death by hanging is thought to have been introduced by the Saxons when they invaded Britain in the fifth century.

Our modern justice system is far from perfect but at the present time we have a lot to be thankful for in comparison to past centuries. Some of us still believe in the death penalty for serious crimes. If one could go back in time and speak to those who were burned at the stake, beheaded, hanged or suffered any such form of execution, they would surely disagree, or would they? Perhaps death would have been the more attractive option in comparison to being incarcerated for life in a hell-hole such as a castle dungeon, a gaol or a lunatic asylum.

Witches have been mentioned as far back as the twelfth century but it was in the seventeenth century that their real persecution took place. Superstition born of ignorance was rife. If hens stopped laying eggs or a cow's milk went sour it was often believed that witchcraft was to blame and the finger would be pointed at someone believed to be the culprit. Most of the condemned witches were elderly women, perhaps with illnesses, such as Alzheimer's disease, that we now understand sometimes come with old age. There were also those who performed 'magic' cures by reciting incantations or using herbs. If one were ill and poor it would be preferential and cheaper to go to one of these mystics rather than a barber-surgeon with his 'tools of torture'. The problem was that if the cure failed the client would then perhaps become vindictive and denounce that person as a witch. This could lead to some poor innocent being degraded in public by being stripped and searched for the Devil's mark, then tried and executed.

Many of the convicted went to their deaths pleading their innocence and there is no doubt that some would have been telling the truth. Before Appeals Courts became established as part of the legal system executions usually took place within a few days of the trial. When mercy was recommended or petitions for reprieve were obtained the case would be put before the Home Secretary. In cases of murder, rape and robbery a reprieve was rarely granted.

Prior to the twentieth century blood grouping and fingerprinting were non-existent. There was no means of establishing whether blood was human or animal, much less matching the group to a particular person. Now, in the twenty-first century, science has forged ahead with modern technology. Forensic evidence in the form of fingerprinting, DNA and other methods have meant that an innocent person can usually be eliminated from any criminal enquiry. Mistakes will always be made because of human error but hopefully the margin for error will become less as time goes on. The system still demands many changes, especially concerning sentences to fit the crime, but hopefully, in the near future, the person on trial will only be found guilty without a shadow of a doubt and the innocent will be freed.

CHAPTER 1

Incarceration and Execution

The gibbet would be erected within sight of the felon's crime demonstrating his fate as a warning to others.

The Castle Keep, which was founded in 1168, has seen horrors far worse than can be imagined. Mainly in cases of treason, it was not uncommon for the heads of executed felons to decorate a major town upon some high focal point to be, hopefully, seen as a deterrent to others contemplating a similar crime. In 1305 when William Wallace was hung, drawn and quartered, his right arm was displayed on the bridge at Newcastle and other unnamed body parts on the Castle walls. In 1323 the walls were host to a quarter of the Earl of Carlisle and in 1415 to the head of Sir Thomas Grey of Wark.

But it was not just the dead that suffered indignities upon and within these grey stone walls. In 1400 Newcastle town became a county taking custody of its own prisoners. Newgate Gaol had been built as part of the town walls. The Keep became the county gaol for Northumberland and Newgate became the town authority gaol.

John Howard, the 'father' of prison reform in the latter quarter of the eighteenth century, conducted a visit of Britain's prisons. Newcastle's Newgate Gaol and the House of Correction received favourable reports. The Castle Keep was a different matter. He was appalled by the conditions there:

Men and women confined together for 7 or 8 nights – in a dirty damp dungeon – having no roof, in wet season is some inches deep. The felons are chained to rings on the wall, shown to the public like wild beasts and the vulgar and curious pay 6d each for admission.

The formidable Castle Keep in the eighteenth century. Over the years numerous heads and limbs have decorated its towers. It has also been the last abode of many a condemned felon. Author's collection

In *An Impartial History of Newcastle upon Tyne* by John Baillie (1801), another insight into the conditions within the Keep was recorded:

> *A man is to be accounted guilty till he is legally proven to be innocent, which is frequently the case. His punishment, viz. being manacled, conveyed through the public streets fixed on a cart, thrown into this den of filth, covered only with a little straw, chained to the wall and shewn like a wild beast to the gaping mob, by a rapacious gaoler at two pence a-piece; his punishment, supposing him acquitted, is only then to cease.*

By the time this was written the practice of allowing the public to view the humiliation of the prisoners had ceased when a new county gaoler was appointed.

As time went on this dank basement was used less and less. For a few days of the year it would accommodate prisoners who

were to appear at the Assizes and condemned prisoners awaiting the death sentence. When Newgate was to be demolished the basement of the Keep, by then the property of the Newcastle Corporation, was used as a short term arrangement to house prisoners until the new gaol was completed and ready to receive inmates. Although Howard's report on Newgate was 'favourable' it would certainly not have come up to modern standards although there were blankets, candles and medical attention

The dungeons within the Castle Keep where felons would be chained to the pillars and the walls whilst awaiting trial and execution. The public could pay a fee to satisfy their morbid curiosity and view the misery and humiliation of the prisoners. Author's collection

supplied, rare commodities for prisoners at that time. Both at the House of Correction and Newgate conditions were cramped and extremely unsanitary. Fevers and illness were common and in some cases fatal.

In 1819 prison reformers Elizabeth Fry and her brother, John Guerney, visited Newgate. Some of their observations were as follows:

The felons in the prison are allowed 5d per day. They are heavily ironed, and may be fastened at the gaoler's pleasure, to an iron ring band fixed into the floor of their cells. The manner in which they are confined is extremely objectionable. Having no access to the yard or any sleeping cells, they pass both day and night in their small day room.

The accommodation for debtors consists of one large day room and six small lodging rooms, without fire places, the doors of the latter opening into the former; also a small court-yard. There is no effectual separation between the men and women debtors. There was, at this time one of the latter descriptions in the gaol. We have seldom observed a female in prison so fearfully exposed to danger.

An inspection by Alderman Reed in 1818 had also deemed the building unsuitable and it was decided to build a new facility. Demolition of Newgate began in 1823 as the new gaol on Carliol Square was being built. The prisoners were moved to the Castle Keep on a temporary basis and from there to their new accommodation in 1828. Within a few years this gaol also became unacceptable because of changing standards and a great increase in the prison population. The practice of sentencing felons to transportation had become less of an option and this added to the problem. Transportation for criminals had almost ceased altogether by 1867.

Morpeth Gaol was used from 1828 chiefly as temporary accommodation for drunks, vagabonds and thieves from Northumberland, although there were three public and two private executions carried out there and the bodies buried within the grounds. One of the local nicknames for the gaol was 'Her Majesty's Temperance Hotel'. On 24 October 1881 Morpeth Gaol closed and its fixtures and fittings were

The forbidding exterior of Newgate Gaol in 1813. Built in the fifteenth century as part of the town walls, the building was demolished in 1823. Author's collection

auctioned off. The building itself was demolished. This closure meant that Newcastle had then to also accommodate Northumberland prisoners. Newcastle Gaol was eventually closed in 1925 after which executions for felons within the area took place at Durham.

In some cases, after an execution, the body would be gibbeted. This entailed the body being covered in pitch and encased in what would have resembled a fitted cage. It would be made from iron bands or chains with the sole purpose of keeping the body intact as long as possible. Where a gallows was usually a permanent fixture at a given spot or a prison, a gibbet was meant as a temporary construction. It would consist of an upright post and a beam from which to hang the body for display. The gibbet would be erected within sight of the scene of the felon's crime demonstrating his fate as a warning to others. Although meant as a temporary fixture it

The entrance gate to Newcastle Gaol, built in Carliol Square in 1823 to replace the old Newgate Gaol. Author's collection

would sometimes take years for a body to rot away completely. A law was passed to end the practice of gibbeting in 1834.

How long gallows were in place on the Town Moor is not known but there are records dating them from 1357 and it is probable they were there long before that year. Hangings were seen by the population as a festive occasion and people would come from miles away to be spectators. Of course the main attraction, and his or her family and friends, would not see it as quite so festive. Hundreds, if not thousands, of people would line the route and congregate around the immediate vicinity of the gallows to watch the doomed felons on the final journey to meet their maker. The wealthiest of the population would pay for rooms in houses and public houses with a good window view of the proceedings. Drink would flow and trouble was inevitable with squabbles breaking out and pickpockets having a field day amongst the crowds. Friday, 23 August 1844 saw the last hanging on the Town Moor.

Another gallows was situated outside the Westgate which was used mainly to execute Northumberland felons. The last person to be hanged here was Thomas Clare on Friday, 16 August 1805. The gallows at Westgate were not removed until 1811. Public hangings still took place on the wall of Newcastle Gaol until a new act was passed ordering all executions to be held in private. The last public execution in Newcastle was that of George Vass on Saturday, 14 March 1863 and the last person to be hanged at Newcastle in a private execution was Ambrose Quinn on Wednesday, 26 November 1919.

Crimes punishable by death once included horse and sheep stealing; highway robbery; arson; rape; riot; burglary; house-

Newcastle from the Rope Walk in Gateshead in 1819. It was in this year that Elizabeth Fry visited Newcastle to inspect Newgate Gaol. Author's collection

breaking; returning from transportation before the sentence had been served; treason and coining. Until the beginning of the nineteenth century all classes, including the gentry, would turn out to see a good execution. Gradually attitudes changed and by the middle of the century it would only be the lower classes that would watch such an event. Laws steadily changed on what was considered a capital crime punishable by death. More prisons were built to house those that previously would have faced the rope or transportation. As the twentieth century dawned campaigning became stronger for an end to the death penalty altogether. August of 1964 saw the last hanging in Britain and in 1968 the death penalty was abolished except for the crime of treason and piracy with violence. This was abolished in 1998 under the Crime and Disorder Act. In 1999 the sixth protocol of the European Convention of Human Rights was signed by the Home Secretary, which ensured that the death penalty had been formally abolished and could not be reinstated.

In the early years, the bodies of executed felons would be handed over to their family or friends to be buried. They could be interred in a churchyard but it was usually on the north side within the shadow of the church. Surgeons were desperate to learn new medical skills and would pay to obtain a fresh human body so grave robbing was a profitable enterprise for those willing to carry out the ghoulish task. St Mary's Church at Morpeth has the unusual addition of a tower that was built in the 1830s to guard against body snatchers robbing the churchyard. The families of those whose graves were desecrated were, understandably, upset. Eventually the Murder Act of 1752 allowed that bodies of executed criminals could be given over to the surgeons for dissection in the belief that this would ease the grave

Elizabeth Fry, a champion of prisoners, visited Newgate Gaol in 1819 and found conditions to be unsatisfactory. Author's collection

robbing situation. As there were only nine bodies handed over in Newcastle within approximately seventy-five years it is doubtful that it had any effect on the finances of the grave robbers. The practice of using hanged felons for medical research was eventually abolished and after 1829 the bodies of those executed at Newcastle were buried within the confines of the gaol. In some cases lime was sprinkled over the bodies to hasten decomposition.

When Newcastle Gaol was to be demolished the fifteen bodies of executed felons that had been buried there were to be moved to Jesmond Cemetery. Only twelve coffins were found with the bodies inside, one of them empty. Perhaps the three missing bodies ended up on a surgeon's table and some of the gaol staff had money in their pockets for a jar or two of ale!

CHAPTER 2

The Executioners

Askern was not particularly competent ... there were many reports of a felon struggling at the end of a rope before death.

Although there were many executioners prior to John 'Jack' Ketch in the seventeenth century, it is he who has gone down in the annals of history with his name being used synonymously to identify with many of the hangmen that succeeded him. Almost any male could be allotted the task of executing their fellow man. The Lord of the Manor or their Bailiff could appoint a worker to do the deed. In many cases the executioner would be a condemned prisoner who would be given the option of a lesser sentence or even freedom if they accepted the appointment. Jack Ketch was one such prisoner being incarcerated for debt at the time. His appointment as executioner was to last twenty-three years with many a felon suffering an unspeakably painful death at his hands. During Ketch's time in office treason was punishable by beheading and it is known that he often did not carry this task out with precision. Whether it was a case of bad aim or the fact that the axe had not been sharpened, in many cases, the hapless person would take many minutes to die as it took more than one attempt before their head was finally hacked off.

Prior to the nineteenth century, although there are records of many early executions at Newcastle, there is sparse information on the individuals who carried out the deed as the name of the executioner was not usually mentioned in any reports. From the seventeenth to the nineteenth century Newcastle employed its own hangman. Alexander Robinson was appointed in 1705, taking over from Thomas Cooper, but no executions took place until 1733, so his time in office

The block and axe in the Tower of London. Beheading was once a popular form of execution (except for those with their heads on the block). Author's collection

would have been spent in whipping felons, meting out other punishments for petty crime and cutting the houghs, or sinews, of swine. This practice stopped the swine running amok in the streets of the town, hence the title that went with the office, Whipper and Hougher. Another who is mentioned was William Gardner, in 1792. He was under sentence of death for sheep stealing and readily agreed when he was offered instead the option of transportation if he would carry out the executions of William Winter, Jane and Eleanor Clark for the robbery and murder of Margaret Crozier. In about 1836, with travelling becoming easier, Newcastle began employing hangmen from elsewhere. In 1844 John Murdoch of Glasgow, aged seventy-six, hanged Mark Sherwood on the Town Moor and in 1850 Nathaniel Howard of York, aged seventy, hanged Patrick Forbes on a scaffold erected in Carliol Square. Both felons had been convicted of murdering their

William Calcraft was in office from 1829–74. This photograph was taken in 1870. Author's collection

wives. Sherwood's was the last hanging to take place on the Town Moor.

Thomas Askern was from York and was in office from 1856–77 and died in 1878. He was about forty and had been imprisoned in York Castle for debt when he took up the post because the regular hangman, William Calcraft, could not carry out an impending execution. Askern was not particularly competent at his work as there were many reports of a felon struggling at the end of the rope before death. In 1863 Askern hanged George Vass for the brutal rape and murder of Margaret Docherty at the West Walls. The scaffold was erected at a corner of Newcastle Gaol facing the steps of the Royal Arcade. This was to be the last public execution in Newcastle and after that year the death sentence was carried out within the walls of the gaol attended only by prison officials, the executioner and his assistants. The first private execution in Newcastle was carried out on 23 December 1875 by William Marwood on John William Anderson for the murder of his wife. Marwood was born at Horncastle in Lincolnshire in 1820. Although a cobbler by trade he took an interest in the method used by the hangmen and felt that he could perform a hanging far more humanely. He is credited with inventing the 'long drop', which meant that if a person's weight was calculated against the length of rope used death would be quicker and therefore less painful for the prisoner and less stressful for those watching. Marwood was fifty-four when he carried out his first hanging and everything went so smoothly that he was appointed official hangman. He performed 176 executions throughout his nine years of service. Marwood died in 1883 of inflammation of the lungs.

James Berry was born at Heckmondwike in Yorkshire in 1852. He was working as a policeman in Bradford when he met William Marwood. Berry, like Marwood, had also worked out tables based on the weight of the prisoner which gradually become more refined. He carried out approximately 200 hangings from 1884–92 when he was in office. For all his attention to detail not all of his hangings went smoothly. At least three prisoners strangled to death, two were very nearly decapitated and one actually was. In another instance, at the

William Marwood was in office from 1874–83 and carried out the executions of Richard Charlton at Morpeth and John Anderson at Newcastle in 1875; and George Hunter at Morpeth in 1876.
Brian Elliott

hanging of John Lee at Exeter, the trap failed to open. After two attempts the prisoner was returned to his cell and later reprieved by the Home Office. Berry felt that they were more humane in their treatment of the condemned in the North than other parts of the country. It was not usually allowed for a prisoner awaiting execution to have any form of close contact with relatives or friends. This was to prevent poison or some other form of means to commit suicide being passed to the doomed person giving them the opportunity to deprive the hangman of his task. When Berry and John Morley came to Newcastle to hang Patrick Judge for the murder of his wife, Judge was allowed physical contact with his friends and his sister. Berry was the first hangman literate enough to write about his work. His book, of which the original has become very rare, was entitled *My Experiences as an Executioner*.

James Billington was born in 1847 at Farnworth in Lancashire. He was appointed hangman for Yorkshire in 1884 and became hangman for London and the Home Counties when Berry retired in 1892. Billington performed 147 executions, the last being in December 1901. He died shortly afterward from pneumonia and was succeeded by his sons. Billington's eldest son, Thomas, was born in 1872 and was in office from 1897 assisting his father and brother until 1902 when he died from pneumonia. William was born in 1873 and held office from 1902–05. He carried out the last execution at Newgate and the first at Pentonville. William died in 1934. John was the youngest of the three Billington boys and was born in 1880. He held office from 1902 until his death in 1905.

John Ellis lived in Rochdale for fifty-eight years. At first he tried manual work but after injuring his back had to seek something less strenuous. His father had owned a hairdressing business which Ellis had never wanted to be part of. Eventually, because his choices of work were limited, he opened a barber's shop in Oldham Road in Rochdale. Somewhere along the line the idea of becoming an executioner came into his head. He wrote to the Governor of Strangeways and was given an interview, training, and ultimately, a job. The pay was £10 per execution and £2.10s

James Berry was in office from 1884 to 1892 and carried out the executions of Patrick Judge in 1886 and William Row in 1890 at Newcastle. Author's collection

(£2.50p) for an assistant. Ellis held the office of executioner from 1901 until March 1924 when he resigned due to poor health. The last execution he performed was on John Eastwood at Leeds in 1923. In all he hanged 203 people, most notably Dr Crippen for the murder of his wife and George Smith who was responsible for the Brides in the Bath murders. In January 1923 Ellis, assisted by Robert Baxter and Thomas Phillips, hanged Edith Thompson for being an accessory to the murder of her husband. She was so distressed that she had to be carried to the gallows. Ellis and William Willis also hanged Susan Newell at Glasgow, the second woman for Ellis in just nine months. Four months later Ellis resigned as executioner. It was known that he disliked hanging women and it is probable that was why he gave up his post, although he told a reporter that was not the reason and that his worst day as an executioner was when he had to hang six men in Ireland, all before breakfast.

After his retirement Ellis wrote his memoirs which were published as *Diary of a Hangman*. Alcohol became a real

John Ellis was in office from 1901 to 1924 and either assisted or carried out the executions at Newcastle of John and John Robert Miller in 1901; Henry Perkins in 1905; Alexander Dickman in 1910; and Ernest Scott and Ambrose Quinn in 1919. Author's collection

problem to Ellis and in 1924 during one of his drinking bouts he tried to shoot himself. He ended up in court charged with attempted suicide, which was, at the time, a criminal offence. He was bound over for twelve months and it was suggested by the judge that he stay away from alcohol. In December 1927 Ellis acted as the executioner William Marwood in a play called *The Adventures of Charles Peace* but his acting career was short lived as the play was considered in such bad taste that it closed after a week. Ellis had kept his hairdressing business but in the 1930s the economy was bleak during the Depression and the shop was not paying its way. He then took to the road, giving demonstrations on executions. While working in London he became ill and had to return home. In 1932 Ellis had a particularly heavy drinking binge. He brandished a razor at his wife, Annie, and his daughter, Amy, threatening to cut their heads off. Austin Ellis, the eldest son, lived nearby and the two terrified women ran to his house. Austin immediately went to his parents' house but he was too late. As he approached, his father was at the front door in the act of cutting his own throat. This time his suicide attempt worked and he died on 20 September 1932 at the age of fifty-eight.

Robert Baxter was born in Hertford and was in office from 1915–35.

Henry Pierrepoint, his brother Thomas, and his son, Albert, were from Clayton near Bradford in West Yorkshire. These three, as did the Billingtons before them, took on the rather bizarre family trade as hangmen. Henry was in office from 1901–10 and carried out 107 executions. Thomas was six

Thomas and Henry Pierrepoint. Henry, along with John Ellis, executed Henry Perkins in 1905 and Thomas carried out the executions of John Amos in 1913 and William Cavanagh in 1917, at Newcastle. Author's collection

years older than Henry and was in office from 1906–46, retiring when he was in his mid-seventies. It is thought he carried out about 300 executions. Thomas and Henry had both worked as assistants with Ellis and said after his suicide that he should have done it earlier as he was impossible to work with. They thought that Ellis had paid far too much attention to detail.

Albert Pierrepoint was in office from 1931–56 and carried out more than 400 executions. On his retirement Albert wrote his memoirs which were published as *Executioner: Pierrepoint.* He had spent more than twenty years carrying out the death sentence on convicted criminals but at some time towards the end of his career, in a mockery of his chosen profession, he decided that capital punishment was not the answer to the prevention of serious crimes. Summing up his thoughts and opinions, at the end of his book he states:

It is said to be a deterrent. I cannot agree. There have been murders since the beginning of time, and we shall go on looking for deterrents until the end of time. If death were a deterrent, I might be expected to know. It is I who have faced them last, young lads and girls, working men, grandmothers. I have been amazed to see the courage with which they take that walk into the unknown. It did not deter them then, and it had not deterred them when they committed what they were convicted for. All the men and women I have faced at that final moment convince me that in what I have done I have not prevented a single murder.

Albert Pierrepoint was Henry's son and followed in the family tradition by becoming an executioner. On his retirement he wrote his memoirs from which a book was published. At the end of his career Albert had decided that capital punishment was no deterrent to serious crimes. Author's collection

William Willis was from Accrington in Lancashire. Between 1906 and 1926 he acted as an assistant at more than 100 executions, retiring due to ill-health. He worked with John Ellis, Robert Baxter and Henry and Thomas Pierrepoint. Willis died in 1939.

Robert Wilson was from Manchester and was in office from 1915–35. Edward Taylor, Henry Pollard and Lionel Mann all acted as assistants on occasions.

CHAPTER 3

Short Accounts of Executions Prior to the Nineteenth Century

At the last moment he [Ewen MacDonald] *tried to throw the executioner off the ladder* [1752].

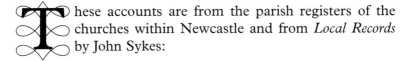hese accounts are from the parish registers of the churches within Newcastle and from *Local Records* by John Sykes:

1306: John de Seyton, one of the esquires of King Robert Bruce, was hanged at Newcastle.

1461: James Butler, Earl of Wiltshire and Ormond, was captured at the Battle of Towton on 29 March and beheaded at Newcastle on 1 May.

1464: The Earl of Kent was beheaded at Newcastle.

1547: On 28 August, 'a newe paire of gallowes' were set up in the market place, and 'a souldier hanged for quarrellying and fighting'.

1564: A person of the name of Partrage was executed for 'coining false money in the great innes in Pilgrim Street'.

1593: Edward Waterson, from London, was executed at Newcastle on 7 January and Joseph Lampton, from Malton in Yorkshire, was executed on 27 July. Both men were Roman Catholic priests.

1599: On 22 August, Clement Roderforthe, gentleman, was executed in the castle and buried at St John's Church.

1602: On 30 July, Robert Brandling, merchant adventurer, was executed and buried at All Saints' Church.

1604: On Monday, 13 August, six prisoners were buried at St Nicholas's Church.

1605: On Thursday, 14 November, three men were hanged at the castle and buried at St John's Church.

1606: On Saturday, 25 January six men were hanged at the castle and buried at St John's Church.

1628: On Tuesday, 19 August, three 'denizens, without names', were hanged for murder and buried at St Nicholas's Church.

1632: On Monday, 13 August, seventeen prisoners were buried at St Nicholas's Church.

1639: On Friday, 13 August, John Anderson, James Browne, George Cranson, Thomas Dabdell, Oswald Browne and Annas Hall were executed and buried at St Nicholas's Church.

1640: On Saturday, 16 May, two soldiers were shot on the Town Moor 'for denying the King's pay'.

1645: On Sunday, 3 August, four men were hanged at the castle, although this is the date recorded it may be incorrect as it was unlikely that executions would take place on a Sunday.

1649: On Tuesday, 3 August, twenty-one men, supposedly border offenders, were executed and buried at St Nicholas Church.

1648: On 30 July George Bruwell, a soldier, executed 'for flying from his collors to the cinime', was executed and buried at St Nicholas's Church.

1701: On Thursday, 25 September, Thomas Leggerton, a wheelwright, was hanged at Newcastle for stabbing a man to death. He was buried in St Andrew's churchyard. On the same day John Fenwick was hanged for murder.

1733: On Monday, 13 August, John Tweddle and Bartholomew Morrison were hanged for unrecorded offences. According to the *Gentlemen's Magazine* these were the first executions to take place at Newcastle for thirty years.

1739: On Tuesday, 4 September, Michael Curry and John Wilson were hanged at the Westgate. Curry had admitted to and been convicted of the murder of Robert Shevil, landlord of the *Three Horseshoes Inn* at Hartley. His body was taken from the Westgate to hang in chains in sight of the scene of his crime. The place where the gibbet was erected became known as Curry's Point.

In 1774 James Maben was convicted of coining. He tried to escape from gaol so was chained to the wall in the dungeon of the castle keep. Author's collection

A sketch by Robert Bertram in 1914 of St Nicholas's Church from the Groat Market. In some cases the parish registers are the only surviving records of executions and burials. Author's collection

John Wilson was convicted of the murder of Barbara, wife of William Trumble, a publican of Dunclawood. Wilson could remember nothing of the murder but supposed he had committed the act during a drunken affray. He was buried in the ground behind St John's churchyard.

1739: On Friday, 14 September, William Smith, aged fifty-three, was hanged on the Town Moor for the murder of his wife. He was said to have made a partial confession to Reverend Wilkinson but withdrew it as the rope was placed around his neck. Smith requested that his clothes be given to his son, a lad of about thirteen, who was present at the execution.

1742: On 24 September, John Todd, for sheep-stealing, and William Simpson, for felony, were executed at Morpeth.

1743: William Brown, known as Sir William Brown by his followers, was tried and received the death sentence at the Newcastle Assizes on Tuesday, 6 August. He had been convicted of stealing at a former Assizes and sentenced to transportation from which he had returned. He pleaded to be transported again and when his request was refused he 'swore foul oaths' at the court. Brown was known to be at the head of a large number of unruly troopers that roamed the area, stealing everything they could lay their hands on. On Thursday, 8 August, two companies of soldiers escorted Brown from the castle to the Westgate, the place of execution, to prevent rescue by his followers.

1744: On Saturday, 11 August, a triple execution took place outside Westgate. James Maben and John Samuel were convicted of coining (forgery), which was considered treason, and Thomas Lister for stealing two black mares. Maben had tried to escape from gaol and when caught was chained to the wall in the dungeon. He was well-educated and, whilst awaiting the sentence of death to be carried out, received visits from many persons of high rank. Maben and Samuel were dressed in white and drawn on a sledge and Lister on a cart, from Newgate Gaol, to the place of execution. All three were buried in St John's churchyard, the two coiners in the same grave.

A sketch by Robert Bertram of St Andrew's Church in 1914. The church dates back to at least the thirteenth century and its churchyard holds the bodies of many executed felons. Author's collection

1746: On Wednesday, 3 September, John Stewart was hanged at Morpeth for burglary of Mr Stokoe's shop in the Castlegarth and also for stealing a horse.

Alexander Anthony was shot on the Town Moor for desertion on Sunday, 15 September.

1751: Richard Brown was fifty-eight and worked as a keelman. He was convicted of the murder of his seventeen-year-old daughter by throwing her down the stairs on 10 November 1750. Brown was hanged on the Town Moor on Wednesday, 21 August 1751. At the gallows he stated that he did not mean to take his daughter's life and, being drunk at the time, did not remember the deed.

1752: On Saturday, 23 May at the *Black Bull Inn* in the Bigg Market run by Mr Pinkney, an argument broke out between Ewen MacDonald, who was quartered at the inn, and some of the customers. MacDonald was

An early sketch of St John's Church and churchyard. To the right of the image a gravedigger stands chatting. Author's collection

nineteen and a new recruit in General Guise's Highlander's regiment. The argument became heated and fists began to fly. Some of the men left the inn and MacDonald followed stabbing one of the men, Robert Parker, in the back of the neck. MacDonald then re-entered the inn and carried on fighting, breaking a man's arm in the process. He was eventually subdued when he was arrested by soldiers. MacDonald later said that two men had come into the inn for a pint of beer and one had begun making remarks against him and his native country of Scotland. In the height of fury and passion he had struck out and stabbed one with a knife. MacDonald had, in his temper, killed the wrong man; it had been Parker's companion that had insulted him.

MacDonald was sentenced to death and hanged on the Town Moor on Thursday, 22 September. John Young, the executioner would have remembered the event as MacDonald did not go to his death easily. At the last moment he tried to throw the executioner off the ladder. After the body was cut down it was taken to the Surgeon's Hall for dissection.

Later reports, whether true or false has never been established, but MacDonald was supposed to have revived whilst on the surgeon's table. A young apprentice surgeon, not wanting to lose a body to practice on, was said to have finally killed MacDonald by hitting him on the head with a mallet. A further report stated that the apprentice was later killed by a kick from a horse. Was this rough justice or MacDonald's ghost?

1754: Dorothy Catenby, a widow, of Love Lane on the Quay, was convicted of murdering her illegitimate child. She was hanged on the Town Moor on Wednesday, 7 August and her body was later taken to the Surgeon's Hall for dissection. Catenby had three lawful children. After her death her two sons drowned themselves and her daughter moved away from the town.

1758: Alice Williamson, aged sixty-eight, was hanged on the Town Moor on Monday, 7 August. She had been caught

Sandgate, where Robert Lindsay was shot by George Stewart in 1764. Stewart was a pawnbroker and thought Lindsay was going to rob him. Author's collection

stealing from a house in the Groat Market belonging to Robert Marshall, a baker. Williamson was described as 'an aged offender'.

William Bland, a soldier, was shot on the Town Moor on Monday, 20 February for desertion.

1761: On Monday, 5 October, Peter Patterson was hanged at Morpeth for High Treason. The rope broke and he was hanged a second time. According to the law, his heart was cut out and burned. Patterson was seventy-four at the time of his death.

1764: On 8 July, at about four o'clock on Sunday morning, Robert Lindsay, a keelman, had climbed onto a wall in an entry in Sandgate. The wall was near to the window of a pawnbroker, George Stewart. Mrs Stewart spotted Lindsay and, thinking that he may have burglary in mind, shouted at him to go. When he refused to leave Mrs Stewart lifted some tongs and, leaning out of the window, struck the intruder two or three times. Lindsay became angry and began breaking panes of glass in the window. George Stewart then took his gun and threatened to shoot Lindsay who still refused to leave. Stewart fired the gun which only flashed. He then told his wife to fetch more powder. Mrs Stewart did as she was bid then primed the gun and handed it back to her husband who promptly fired it again. This time the shot found its mark and Lindsay was killed. Stewart and his wife were arrested and committed to Newgate Gaol. At the Assizes George Stewart was convicted of murder. He was hanged on the Town Moor on Monday, 27 August and his body taken to the Surgeon's Hall for dissection.

In the same year, on Monday, 3 September, James Edgar was hanged at the Westgate for burglary and larceny. He had been tried at the August Assizes for breaking into the house of Edward Bigge at West Jesmond. Edgar, a cobbler, Thomas Harrison, a hawker, Isabella, Harrison's partner and her eight-year-old son, Alexander Simpson were caught at Sandgate on 6 January. On a search being made of Edgar's house, where Harrison and his partner lodged, the goods that had been stolen were found. Edgar admitted to the crime saying that Harrison and his partner had put the young boy through the window of the house first and then Isabella had gone in and handed the goods out to Harrison and himself. Edgar was convicted and the others acquitted.

1765: On Thursday, 15 August, Joseph Hall, a soldier of the 6th Regiment of Foot, was hanged at Morpeth for highway robbery. On 11 September 1764 Hall had attacked Mr Cuthbertson, a hairdresser as he returned home from Gosforth in a post-chaise. Hall had fired a pistol leaving the driver with severe burns to his face. The horses had taken fright and bolted. When Mr Cuthbertson and the driver managed to calm the horses they procured help to track down the robber. Hall meanwhile, had tried to rob another two men on horse-back but they had managed to gallop away from him.

1774: On Saturday, 16 August George Davidson was hanged at Morpeth for rape.

1776: In October of 1775 Robert Knowles, the North Shields postman, stole a letter containing two £50 notes from the Newcastle post office. The money was the property of Robert Rankin, a merchant. Knowles was arrested on 13 November 1775 and was incarcerated in Newgate Gaol. On the night of 1 June 1776 he feigned illness. The turnkey, feeling sorry for the prisoner, did not put Knowles in irons as was customary but only locked him in his cell. When the turnkey did his hourly rounds he saw a bundle lying in the cell which Knowles said was foul linen. The turnkey bent over to examine the bundle and as he did so Knowles slipped out of his cell and locked the turnkey in. Twenty guineas were offered as a reward leading to the escaped prisoner's apprehension and on 6 June he was re-captured when he was seen by pitmen at Walker Colliery.

Knowles was executed on the Town Moor on Wednesday, 21 August 1776. The gallows were erected on the ground of an old pit heap and during the execution, where some of the onlookers were standing, the ground gave way beneath them. Horses bolted in panic and many people were knocked over but, apart from a few bruises, there were no injuries sustained.

On the same day Andrew MacKenzie was hanged at the Westgate. He had robbed a man named Temple on the Shields Road. During this execution a butcher, William Robson, dropped dead beside the gallows, probably due to a heart attack. He may have wanted to

St Andrew's Church in 2003. Executed felons were usually buried in the shadows, at the north side of the church. The author

witness both executions and had over-exerted himself running from the Town Moor to Westgate. Robson got more of his share of death than he bargained for.

1783: William Alexander was hanged on Monday, 17 November on the Town Moor for forgery and afterwards buried at St Andrew's Church.

1784: James Chambers, a Scotsman, and William Collins, an Irishman, were convicted of robbing Mr Jasper Anderson of Coxlodge, near to his house on 18 November 1783. They were hanged on Friday, 27 August on the Town Moor. Both bodies were buried in the same grave at St Andrew's Church.

1785: On Tuesday, 16 August, William Cockburn and William Graham were hanged at Morpeth for horse-stealing.

1786: Henry Jennings, a yeoman, was hanged on the Town Moor on Wednesday, 30 August for horse-stealing. He was buried at St Andrew's Church. During the execution a boy, Peter Donnison, was caught picking the pocket of Thomas Brown, a millwright, who was standing at the foot of the gallows. Shortly afterwards Andrew Donaldson, a glover and breeches maker, was caught with his hand in a cordwainer's (Thomas Hamilton's) pocket. A constable was called and Donaldson was taken before the Mayor.

1788: John Winter and Robert Winter, father and son, were hanged at Morpeth on Wednesday, 6 August. They were sentenced to death for breaking in to the house of the Charlton family at Hesleyside.

1789: Twenty-four-year-old Thomas Young was hanged at Morpeth on Wednesday, 16 August, for highway robbery.

1790: Thomas Watson was single and lived with his father on a farm at Elford. He had been firm friends with George Gibson who was married and lived on a farm at Coldrife in Northumberland. Watson heard that Gibson had accused him of unnatural crimes and, becoming incensed with anger, went to Alnwick and purchased a pistol, balls and powder. On the night of 19 February he went to a local tavern and filled himself with alcohol then laid in wait at a spot he expected Gibson to pass. His intended victim did not appear at night. The following morning Watson went to Gibson's farm and shot him through the heart. At the trial held at the Moot Hall before Baron Thompson a plea of temporary insanity was put forward. There was no evidence to substantiate this so Watson was sentenced to death. He was hanged on Thursday 5 August at the Westgate and his body was taken to the Surgeon's Hall for dissection. During the trial, Jane Stephenson, was caught stealing a handkerchief out of a young man's pocket. She was duly arrested, tried and sentenced to seven years' transportation. This all took place in a matter of minutes.

At Morpeth, on Wednesday, 18 August a triple execution took place. Those hanged were John Brown for house-breaking at Fenham, James Greenwood for shop-breaking at North Sunderland and George Bolton for horse-stealing.

1792: On Wednesday, 22 August a triple execution took place at Morpeth. Those hanged were Sylvester Broadwater for stealing a mare with a value of £20 at Brampton, Joseph Marshall for stealing a mare with a value of £10 at Brampton and Christopher Taylor for arson and robbery at Bardon Mill.

1793: Walter Clarke, aged fifty, for burglary and stealing clothing at Wooler and Margaret Dunn, aged forty-five, for burglary, stealing clothing, gold and silver at Corbridge, were hanged at Fair Moor, Morpeth on Wednesday, 14 August.

CHAPTER 4

Short Accounts of Nineteenth Century Executions

... he became so agitated ... it was said he was 'nearly dead' by the time he reached the gallows.

1801: John Scott was hanged at Morpeth on Thursday, 19 November for sheep-stealing.

1805: On Sunday, 19 August 1804 two drummers and a private belonging to the 2nd Staffordshire Militia were out in the early hours of the morning to collect mushrooms in a field near Cullercoats. They heard what

The Westgate, where Northumberland felons were executed. The last execution at Westgate was that of Thomas Clare in 1805. The gallows were demolished in 1811. Author's collection

they thought were cries of distress and followed the sound to investigate. In a field they found a man's hat which one of them recognised as belonging to Thomas Clare, a private in their regiment. At that moment a soldier appeared in front of them and, jumping over the hedge, ran towards their camp. The three men carried on walking across the field when they saw the body of a man lying in a ditch. They went back to the camp and reported what they had seen to the sergeant. Clare was immediately placed under arrest.

The dead man was William Todd, a pitman, who was fifty and had a wife and seven children. A piece of rail that was covered in blood was found near to the body. The man had been badly beaten about the body and face and had sustained broken ribs.

Clare was convicted of Todd's murder and hanged at the Westgate on Friday, 16 August 1805, at the age of twenty-one. He never admitted to his guilt and became so agitated when watching the preparations for his execution it was said that he was 'nearly dead' by the time he reached the gallows. Clare was the last person to be hanged at the Westgate. The gallows remained standing until 1811.

1808: Martin O'Bryan was hanged at Morpeth on Thursday, 1 September for robbing and cutting the throat of Barbara Weir upon the Shields road.

1809: On Saturday, 19 August, John Boyd was hanged at Morpeth for forgery. He was twenty-one and had assumed an alias so that his family and friends in Ireland were not embarrassed by his fate.

1816: James O'Neill, an Irishman, robbed George Angus, a carrier, of Mickley, on the highway as he was returning from the preceding October Cow Hill fair. O'Neill was hanged on the Town Moor on Saturday, 7 September 1816 at the age of twenty-three. His body was conveyed by his friends to a public house near the gaol, where it was 'waked'. On Sunday the body was interred in St Andrew's churchyard. About thirty Irish people were at the grave.

1819: Joseph Charlton, aged twenty-four, was hanged at Morpeth on Wednesday, 14 April 'for an unnatural crime'. He was interred near Tynemouth Priory with around 2,000 people present.

1821: John Wilkinson and William Surtees Hetherington were hanged at Morpeth on Monday, 10 September, for robbing William Nesbit of Long Benton as he returned home from Newcastle.

1822: Mark Lawson and William Currie, both from Northumberland, were hanged at Morpeth on Wednesday, 20 March, for robbing Henry Thompson at South Lodge near Gosforth.

1825: On Monday, 20 June, William Probert, William Sargent, alias Barker, and Harper for horse-stealing and Smith for burglary, all hanged at Newgate.

The ruins of Tynemouth Priory near to where Joseph Charlton was interred after his execution in 1819. Author's collection

CHAPTER 5

The Newcastle Witch Hunt 1650

The test was carried out by sticking a pin into various parts of the body.

On 26 March 1649 a petition was handed to the Newcastle Common Council concerning fears about witchcraft being practised. Where this petition originated is unknown but it is thought it was from the inhabitants of Newcastle. The magistrates sent Thomas Shevell and Cuthbert Nicholson, two of their sergeants, to Scotland to speak with a man who professed to be able to detect witches. In July of 1649 a witch-finder had been sent for by the officials of the town of Berwick:

Ordered that, according to the Guild's desire, the man which tryeth the witches in Scotland shall be sent for, and satisfaction be given him by the towne in defraying his charges, and in coming hither, and that the towne shall engage that no violence be offered him by any person within this towne.

It is likely that this Scotsman, whose name remains a mystery as it was unrecorded, was the same man that was later sent for to carry out his work in Newcastle. On the witch-finder's arrival in Newcastle, in December 1649, a bell-ringer was sent through the streets to deliver the message that any who had a complaint against someone they thought guilty of witchcraft would be brought before the witch-finder to be tested. As a consequence thirty women were brought to the town hall to be 'pricked' to see if they were witches. This test was carried out by sticking a pin into various parts of the body. If the wound did not bleed that person was declared guilty of witchcraft:

A woman being examined in public by pinpricking, to determine whether she is a witch. Author's collection

> *That many witches were apprehended thereabouts of late; that the witch-tryer taking a pin and thrusting it into the skin in parts of their bodies, they were insensible of it, which is one circumstance of proof against them.*

The witch-finder was to be paid 20s (£1) for each witch that he exposed. He could become very wealthy so would be, no doubt, expert in his task. The pin would, perhaps, have been thrust into a raised skin blemish, such as a wart, or perhaps a blunt pin was used. Mass hysteria amongst those believing in witchcraft would bind them to a person they would consider above reproach, using any form of trickery. The witch-finder also claimed he could tell a witch by her looks. Two of the women were exonerated and allowed to return to their homes. One of the suspects was perhaps younger and better looking than the rest. When it became her turn to be examined the witch-finder drew her clothes right up. A flush crept up throughout her body and she did not bleed when the pin was thrust into her. One of the overseers of the examinations was a Lieutenant Colonel Hobson who thought that this could have been caused by a combination of fear and embarrassment. He ordered the woman to be tested again and this time blood oozed from the wound so she was declared innocent. Twenty-seven of the women tested were found guilty

An illustration of the execution of the witches at Newcastle. Author's collection

and incarcerated to await their trials. They would probably have been held at Newgate Gaol.

The witch-finder left Newcastle for Durham where at least two more women were declared 'children of the Devil'. He then carried on do his work in Northumberland where he was paid £3 for each person 'proved' to practise witchcraft. A Justice of the Peace, Henry Ogle, was not taken in by the witch-finder's claims and wanted him arrested. The villain managed to escape and returned to Scotland. His freedom did not last for long as he was arrested there and eventually met his death on the gallows. Before he was sent to meet his Maker he confessed to have been the instrument of death of more than 220 women in England and Scotland.

The records of the witch trials have not survived but some of these poor souls were certainly found guilty. In August 1650 the hangman was kept busy on the Town Moor. In all, about sixteen individuals found guilty of witchcraft met their deaths at the end of a rope. On the same day ten others were hanged for stealing. This, at that time, would have meant death by slow strangulation. In the register of St Andrew's parochial chapelry, dated Saturday, 21 August 1650, there is a list of those that were hanged that day and buried in unmarked graves in St Andrew's churchyard. There are the names of fifteen women and one man executed as witches, one woman for stealing and the nine moss troopers (lawless groups who roamed the area taking anything they could lay their hands on) convicted of stealing:

The 21 Day of August thes partes her under named were executed in the town mor for wiches

Isabell Brown the 21 day for a wich
Margrit Maddeson the 21 day for a wich
Ann Watson the 21 day for a wich
Ellenor Henderson the 21 day for a wich
Ellenor Rogers the 21 day for a wich
Elsabeth Dobson the 21 day for a wich
Mathew Boulmer the 21 day for a wich
Elsabeth Anderson the 21 day for a wich

St Andrew's churchyard in 2003. It was in this churchyard that the 'witches', hanged in 1650, were buried in unmarked graves. The author

Jane Hunter the 21 day for a wich
Jane Koupling the 21 day for a wich
Margrit Brown the 21 day for a wich
Margrit Moffet the 21 day for a wich
Ellenor Robson stellin of silver spoones
Katren Welsh the 21 day for a wich
Aylles Hume the 21 day for a wich
Marie Pootes the 21 day for a wich

The same day prisoners executed in the towne mor belonging to the Kastle

John Ridley the 21 day for stelling
Simond Armstrong the 21 day for stelling
George Armstrong the 21 day for stelling
Ellot the 21 day for stelling
William Brown the 21 day for stelling
Johnson the 21 day for stelling
John Armestron the 21 day for stelling
Jo. Dronwell the 21 day for stelling
Jane Martin, the miller's wife of Chattin 'for a wich'

CHAPTER 6

A Family Feud
1701

Forster was a proud but quiet man while Fenwick was rather arrogant and opinionated.

The families of Fenwick and Forster were two of the most powerful and revered in Northumberland. The Fenwicks held a family seat at Wallington and the Forsters were given the manor and castle of Bamburgh by James I. They held Bamburgh until 1715 when they lost their lands during the Jacobite Rebellion. Some of the members of these two very important families did not see eye to eye over political matters which caused serious conflict between them.

In August 1701, Ferdinando Forster, MP for Northumberland and John Fenwick of Rock Hall near Alnwick, were called upon to sit upon the Grand Jury of the Assizes at Newcastle. Both men were aged about thirty-one. Forster was single and Fenwick married with his wife pregnant at this time. On 22 August the members of the Grand Jury attended a dinner held at the best inn in Newcastle, the *Black Horse,* which was situated on the west side of Newgate Street.

The two men were of very different personalities. Forster was a proud but quiet man while Fenwick was rather arrogant and opinionated. There is more than one version of the events that followed and as they differ there is controversy as to the circumstances regarding what took place that evening and the following day. One account recorded in John Brand's *History of Newcastle* (1789), was that during the dinner, an argument broke out between the two men concerning their differences of opinion, perhaps over land or politics of the time, and John Hall of Otterburn, on Fenwick's behalf, challenged Forster to a fight. Protocol would have been followed by 'taking their argument' outside. As they left the inn or just as they got

Wallington Hall, Northumberland, once the seat of the Fenwicks. Author's collection

outside Forster tripped and fell. As he lay on the ground Fenwick was said to have taken his opportunity and stabbed Forster where he had fallen.

The other account was written by Alderman Hugh Hornby, to John Brand, suggesting that his version was incorrect. Hornby stated that he had a different version related by respectable people who had lived at that time or soon after. One was Edward Collingwood, Recorder of Newcastle, and Hornby felt that his story was the truthful one. Collingwood's father had been present at the dinner and had told his son that the arrogant Fenwick had entered the inn singing a favourite party song, Sir John Fenwick's *The Flower Among Them*. This had upset Forster and a quarrel took place between the two men. The rest of the company managed to quieten the situation and this should have been the end of the matter but the two men met, quite by accident, near the White Cross the following morning. They began arguing again, swords were drawn, and Forster was killed. Under British law duels were illegal so even if Forster was killed in what would be thought of as a fair fight it would still be classed as murder. Whatever the circumstances of Forster's death, Fenwick would have known he was in dire straits and he quickly made his escape. The fugitive was soon found hiding in a garden either in Gallowgate or Sidgate. He was arrested and charged with Forster's murder. Fenwick then appeared at the same Assizes before the Grand Jury at the Guildhall that he had earlier sat upon amongst his peers. This same Grand Jury then had the

Bamburgh Castle, once the seat of the Forsters. They lost their power and lands in 1715 during the Jacobite Rebellion. Author's collection

Part of Newgate Street as it would have been when Forster and Fenwick met up and fought with swords in 1701. Author's collection

unenviable task of finding Fenwick guilty of murder. As the law demanded, sentence of death was passed.

On 25 September, the day of the execution, all the gates of the town were closed and guarded in case of a rescue attempt by the people of the north who were loyal to Fenwick, especially the pitmen whom he employed at Kenton Colliery. There were no disturbances and Fenwick was hanged on a gallows erected between the White Cross (removed in 1808) and a thorn tree which stood upon Newgate Street. It was customary for a murderer to be hanged looking towards the scene of his crime. Hornby also thought this was wrong and that Fenwick had been hanged from a piece of timber between Newgate Gaol and the gaoler's house. Fenwick was buried in St Andrew's churchyard and Forster at Bamburgh Parish Church. The executions of Fenwick and Thomas Leggerton, who was hanged on the same day for murder, were probably carried out by Thomas Cooper who was the hangman for the town at that time. Leggerton was also buried in St Andrew's churchyard.

CHAPTER 7

Winter & the Teenage Girls
1792

After hanging the customary hour, the bodies of the girls were taken to Surgeon's Hall.

Margaret Crozier was a woman past middle age who occupied a portion of the Pele House (built originally as protection against the Border Rievers) at the Raw in Elsdon. Part of her accommodation was given to a small shop from which she sold drapery goods to the local community. As a shopkeeper she was well-known and very much respected in the district.

On Monday night, 29 August 1791, Margaret was visited by Mary Temple and Elizabeth Jackson. Mary was renowned for her needlework and Elizabeth's father farmed the land around the Pele House. The two young women had called in for a chat before bedtime. As they were leaving they heard dogs barking around a pile of hay that lay a short distance from the house. Mary and Elizabeth left with a warning to Margaret to bolt her door before retiring for the night. Margaret replied, laughingly, that she had nothing to fear as it was probably one of Bessie's (Elizabeth's) sweethearts hiding in the hay waiting to see her.

The following morning Barbara Drummond, a neighbour, arrived at the Pele House to buy some commodity from Margaret. When she arrived at the door she noticed some thread lying on the ground outside. This gave her a sense of foreboding so instead of entering the house she went in search of someone to advise her. On finding Elizabeth Jackson and William Dodds, a joiner, they said they had not seen Margaret that morning and that in itself was unusual. The three neighbours went to the Pele House to make sure everything was well. On reaching the house they found the door shut but

The Pele House at Raw as it was in 1791 when Margaret Crozier was murdered in her bed and robbed by William Winter and the two Clark girls. Author's collection

unlocked. Margaret was lying on her bed with no sign of life. There was a gash to her throat but the wound did not look severe enough to have caused her death. Around her neck and covering part of her face a handkerchief was tied. One of her hands was badly cut as if she had held it up to try and defend herself and the attacker had slashed at her palm. In amongst the bedclothes there was a gully knife stained with blood. Just outside the door there was a plough coulter. It was this instrument which had been used to pry open the bolted door. There was also the imprint of a shoe or boot in the mud. The shop and living accommodation had been ransacked. Many of Margaret's customers were also her friends who would spend some considerable time in the little shop passing the time of day. Because of this fact it could be ascertained that wearing apparel, muslins, drapery and handkerchiefs were missing and accurate descriptions could be given of the articles that had been stolen.

Neighbours from both nearby and several miles away rallied around to try and catch the perpetrators of this despicable crime on their friend and a valued member of the community. The officers of the Parish of Elsdon offered a reward of £5 for information leading to the conviction of the murder or murderers.

On the day prior to the murder two boys had been in a field above the Whitlees farm house and had seen a man and two women sitting in the field eating mutton. Their ass was grazing nearby. One of the boys, Richard Hindmarsh from Whiskerfield farm, had noticed that the man was cutting the meat with a gully knife that was secured to the haft by an iron hoop soldered with brass. When the three strangers had finished eating the man had been sitting on the ground with his legs stretched out and singing a song. Richard later said that he had a clear view of the soles of the man's shoes and the number of nails that were in them. Richard mentioned what he had seen to William Marshall who was in the area to attend the inquest. Marshall in turn told the coroner who halted the inquest until he spoke to the two boys. When young Richard was shown the knife that was found in Margaret's bed he said it was the same as the one he had seen being used to cut

The Moot Hall in 1809. At this time it was in a poor state of repair and was demolished in 1810. The trial of William Winter and the Clark girls was held here in 1792. Author's collection

mutton in the field. Richard also said the man's shoes corresponded with the footprint found at the Raw. Other people in the neighbourhood had also seen the three strangers wandering around on the day prior to the murder. On the day following they were seen driving a loaded ass towards Harlow Hill. The man was described as being about six feet tall with long dark hair tied in a club. He was wearing a light coat, light blue breeches and grey stockings. The two women were described as being tall and stout and dressed in grey cloaks, black bonnets and one had on a light coloured cotton gown.

Arrangements were made for three police constables from Woodside and Elsdon to pursue the suspects. Mounted on horseback, John Brown, William Hall and William Tweedy headed towards Tyneside. On passing Harlow Hill in a dingle called Whittle Dean they came across a man fitting the description of the person they were seeking. They called upon some labourers working in a nearby field to assist them in arresting the man but there was no trouble and their captive came quietly. Near to Ovingham they arrested a woman who denied knowing the male prisoner. This denial was refuted by a dog that was with her. When the dog saw the man it ran to him and fawned all over him so the two parties had to admit they were acquainted. The constables took both their prisoners to Netherwitten to be questioned by Justice of the Peace W Trevelyan but he was not available. The party carried on to Mitford and were brought before B Mitford who was also a Justice of the Peace. The male prisoner was identified as William Winter. There were found to be blood stains on his shirt. Winter explained this fact by saying that he had been fighting but it was thought if this were true he would have removed his shirt so as not to damage or stain it. The two suspects were incarcerated in Morpeth Gaol on Saturday, 3 September. Two more females were arrested soon after, at Barley Moor in Tynedale.

Elizabeth Jackson recalled that the elder of the three women arrested had been in Margaret Crozier's shop in July and they had not liked the way she had been looking around the goods. The three women prisoners were the mother and two daughters of the Clark family. All three often went under the alias of Gregg and were known to belong to a Faw Gang, as did William Winter.

Winter, who was probably of gypsy descent, had been sentenced to seven years on the hulk, on the Thames, in 1784 for horse-stealing and on his release at the beginning of August in 1791 had returned to the North-East of England. Prior to his seven year sentence he had spent only a short time at liberty having committed and been caught for many crimes throughout his life. Winter came from a family of law-breakers as his father, John, and brother, Robert, had been hanged at Morpeth in 1788 for breaking and entering.

At this time the Assizes were only held once a year, in August, in the Northern Counties. The four suspects were left to cool their heels in Morpeth Gaol for nearly a year until the following Assizes. This gave plenty of time to gather evidence against them.

The trial took place at the Moot Hall in August 1792 before Mr Trevelyan and lasted approximately sixteen hours. Two of the women, when arrested, had been in possession of articles of clothing stolen from the Pele House. Richard Hindmarsh, who was about eleven at the time the trial took place, gave his evidence. Winter admitted to the robbery but said that Margaret was still alive when he left. He had sent the two young women back to the house to make sure their victim could not call for help before they made their escape. The girls went back to the house and when they caught up with Winter one of them had said she would not be able to call for help because they 'had tied her up by the meat' which was an expression meaning tying up a horse using a bridle or halter so it cannot eat. Perhaps murder had not been the intention but Margaret Crozier had died from suffocation as a result of the handkerchief being tied around her face and throat to prevent her from calling out. She had also suffered a fractured skull so even if she had not suffocated would probably have died from the head injury.

The outcome of the trial was that the elder Jane Clark was released without charge. It was well-known that she encouraged her family to steal and was thought by many that she had probably planned the robbery but there was no factual evidence to collaborate this. The younger Jane and Eleanor Clark, both still in their teens, were sentenced to be hanged and their bodies given to the surgeons for dissection. William Winter was to be hanged and his body gibbeted in chains near to the spot where the murder was committed. A story that was circulated after the trial was that as the sentences were pronounced one of the girls fainted. Although Winter was heavily ironed he scooped the unconscious girl into his arms and carried her towards the door of the courtroom. As he passed a sympathiser he was handed a half gallon of ale and he left the room carrying his two burdens across the open space to the old castle where the three condemned murderers would be chained to the walls, in separate cells, to await their fate. It

The Hall of the Barber Surgeons where the bodies of the Clark girls were taken for dissection after their execution. Author's collection

is doubtful whether this knight in shining armour story was true as the two girls were about to be hanged partly because of Winter's evidence.

On Friday, 10 August, the three prisoners were placed in a cart and conveyed from the castle and through the Westgate where a gallows had been erected. The executioner was William Gardner, a prisoner also under sentence of death, who had been agreeable to his sentence being changed to seven years transportation instead of hanging if he would carry out the triple execution. Although Winter had admitted guilt to the robbery the two girls protested their innocence until the end. Their protests fell on deaf ears and all three met their deaths within a short space of time. After hanging the customary hour the bodies of the girls were taken to the Surgeon's Hall. The surgeon who performed the dissections later revealed that, although they had lived a life having no morals or scruples, one of the girls had still been a virgin when she died. Later, in 1793, Walter Clark, the father of the two girls, was hanged for burglary.

When Winter's body was cut down it was placed on a long cart and taken to Steng Cross on Whiskershields Common, a few miles from Elsdon. He was left wearing the clothes he had died in. His face was covered and bands of iron were bound around his limbs and chest. At the top of the head the bands were connected with a swivel which was attached to the short beam projecting from the higher part of the upright shaft forming the gibbet. When the body was in place it swung some thirty feet high. This gruesome spectacle was visited by thousands. As time went on the smell became so bad that even horses shied away from the spot. As the body decomposed it was said that the skull was given to Mr Darnell of Newcastle. Eventually, the remaining bones were put in a sack that was tarred inside and out to resist the weather. In time this, too, rotted away and shepherds buried the bones that fell. In the 1860s Sir Walter Trevelyan of Wallington arranged for a wooden replica to be suspended from the beam. The wooden body was used for target practice and small pieces were cut away from both the body and the gibbet in the belief that rubbing the wood on gums would cure toothache. To this day the gibbet still stands with a replica head swinging in the wind to remind all not to follow the path of William Winter as this could be their fate. Near to this site the remains of what is thought to be the base of a Saxon cross was found. It was probably in place to mark the highest point on a drove road that was used to walk the cattle from Scotland to the markets in England. This large stone now sits at the bottom of the gibbet and the entire eerie memorial is under the care of the National Trust and is often depicted in tourist brochures.

Winter's Gibbet keeps a lonely vigil as a stark reminder of past punishments. The monument is now advertised in brochures as a tourist attraction and is cared for by the National Trust. Author's collection

There was a fear that, after the executions, the boy, Richard Hindmarsh, would be in danger from Winter's friends looking to wreak their revenge on him. Mr Trevelyan took him under his protection where he remained as a servant for several years. He was attacked one day coming back from Morpeth and it was only the fact that he had a very fast horse he was able to make his escape. Mr Trevelyan then sent him to live with Reverend Johnson at Bywell but it was still considered that he was in danger so he was taken to live near Aberdeen with Colonel Baird. About eighteen months later he became seriously ill so returned to Whiskershield to be nursed by his father. Richard died of his illness in 1803 at the age of twenty-two.

Look where yon waste
Slopes downward to the south, amongst the tree:
Close by the steading of a farm, thou 'lt mark
A little gable, which the radiant sun
Tips with his glory; 'twas in yonder spot
The murder foul was done. And on that ridge,
Eastward about a mile or more, the pole
With angular arm, which thou seest standing fair
Between us and the sky, tells you the place
Where hung the murderer's body. 'Tis a tale,
Solemn and sad, revealing much of ill,
And vengeance too, without a single trait
Of all-redeeming mercy.

CHAPTER 8

The Revenge of the Pitmen
1795

*A dispute arose between the pitmen and the
serving girl ...*

Thomas Nicholson, who was a pitman of twenty-
three years of age, stood trial on 6 August 1795 for
the murder of Thomas Purvis, a carver and gilder,
and was found guilty. On 21 June, which was Race Sunday,
Purvis was in a tent on the Town Moor when Thomas
Nicholson, a pitman who worked at Bigg's Main Colliery, and
his brother, John, came into the tent for a drink. They joined
the company of a group of other pitmen with whom they were
acquainted. A dispute arose between the pitmen and the
serving girl as to how many drinks they owed for. They were
refusing to pay the sum that she was asking. Purvis intervened
and spoke to the men who eventually paid what they owed and
left the tent. They were angry at the interference and after a
short while they returned bringing another few men with
them. They jeered, taunted and made threats against Purvis.
John Wallis, a police constable, was called to diffuse the
situation and the pitmen eventually left, still hurling abuse and
uttering threats.

When Purvis left the tent later that night some of the pitmen
were waiting and, seizing the opportunity of the object of their
anger being on his own, attacked the defenceless man. The
attackers ran off when two passers by approached but by then
Purvis was so badly beaten that he was near to death. He was
taken to his home in Pilgrim Street but after suffering
considerable agony died of his injuries on the following
Sunday.

A poster for the apprehension of the pitmen involved was
printed and distributed around the area. Eventually five men

were arrested for the attack, including Thomas Nicholson, who was found at Berwick-on-Tweed. The men were incarcerated at Newgate Gaol to await trial.

At the trial two of the men gave evidence for the Crown and two were found not guilty. Nicholson was found guilty of the murder of Purvis and hanged at the Gallows Hole on the Town Moor on Saturday, 8 August. His body was afterwards taken to the Surgeon's Hall for dissection. Thomas Purvis was buried at Ballast Hills cemetery.

CHAPTER 9

Death of a Watchman
1817

... they found a stick that was stained with what was assumed to be blood.

Ouseburn Pottery Works near Newcastle was owned by Mr Dalton. In November of 1816 a repossession order was put into place and the work at the pottery was suspended. A sheriff's officer, John Charlton, was placed in charge of selling off the items within the pottery to pay the debts. Charlton employed Charles Stuart to look after the premises and any money taken from the sales. Stuart lived and slept in an office at the far end of a warehouse. The money was kept within a drawer in a desk within the office, or counting house as it was called. A flight of steps outside led to the door of the warehouse which was bolted at night from the inside by Stuart.

Sometime during the night or morning between 3 and 4 December Stuart answered a knock on the warehouse door and was confronted by two men. The men set about beating Stuart to within an inch of his life. About five o'clock the following morning Jane Buckham and Thomas Pasmore were passing the pottery when they saw Stuart at the upstairs window trying to attract attention to his plight. William Wilkinson, foreman of the pottery, was sent for. On his arrival at about 5.30am it was to find Stuart badly beaten and barely alive. The office had been ransacked and paper and letters littered the floor. A kiln poker was found on one of the stairs leading to the warehouse and it was assumed this had been used to force open the desk to get at the £6 that had been in a locked drawer. Stuart told Wilkinson that he had been attacked by two men, one of whom he could not identify but he said the other was Charles Smith who he had recognised 'by his broad Irish accent and his size'. Stuart was taken to the Newcastle Infirmary and Wilkinson alerted Charlton, the bailiff, as to what he had been told. Wilkinson, Charlton, PC Percival Allen, Joseph Dalton and a few other men went to arrest Smith.

Charles Smith was married with children and had lived originally in Sunderland. He had been in the army but left and had taken employment at the Fulwell Lime Works before becoming a pan-man at the pottery. He was living in lodgings in Stepney Square which was situated only a short distance from the pottery. Smith had still been in bed when the group of men burst into his room at about 7am. When they told Smith why they were there he denied any part in the attack saying he had gone to bed before nine o'clock the previous evening. Smith sat on the bed and began to get dressed. As he was doing this he bent down so his hand was under the bed for a second or two. One of the men present noticed this and, thinking Smith was trying to hide something, reached under the bed pulling out a shoe. Someone mentioned that when Smith had been seen out and about the previous evening he had been wearing top boots (boots that came to the knee) and not shoes. A stain that may have been blood was then seen on one of his boots. Smith said that he had killed a hen a few nights previously so it could have been hen's blood. The other boot was clean. Stains were also noticed on Smith's stockings and breeches. The men took Smith to the infirmary to confront Stuart. Stuart accused Smith of hitting him with some sort of iron weapon then dragging him along the floor of the warehouse into the office and covering his face with part of his own clothing. Smith carried on with his denial that he had been involved. A statement as to what had occurred at the pottery concerning the robbery was written out and read to Stuart, which he then signed.

Meanwhile some of the men had returned to Smith's lodgings where they found a stick that was stained with what they assumed to be blood. The stick was shown to Smith and he said he had used it to kill the hen so if the stains were blood it was hen's blood. Smith was charged with the robbery and the boot, stockings and stick were taken for safe-keeping by

The groined archway of Newgate showing the preparations for the execution of Charles Smith in 1817. He was taken from here by cart to the Town Moor. Author's collection

PC Allen. Stuart's condition deteriorated and he died on 24 December. The charge against Smith then became murder.

At Smith's initial trial there was no shortage of witnesses to point the finger of guilt at him. William Richardson stated that he had seen Smith between seven and eight o'clock in Stepney Square and again at ten o'clock walking towards the pottery. He had been wearing a glazed hat and top boots. When questioned by the defence, Mr Alderson, Richardson admitted only knowing Smith by sight and the man he saw at ten o'clock was a good distance away but was wearing a glazed hat. Alderson then pointed out that the type of hat was very common in Newcastle. James Dowling lived in Stepney Square and said that on the night in question he had heard two men with Irish accents whispering in the gloss kiln of the pottery. Thinking it strange he had stopped to listen and heard one man say 'Will this do?' The other man had replied 'Hush, don't talk so loud or we shall be heard'. Alderson asked if Dowling knew that Stuart was sleeping on the pottery premises and if so then why had he not told him about the conversation if he thought it suspicious. Dowling answered that he did know that Stuart was sleeping in the office but just did not think to tell him about what he had heard. Alderson pointed out that a large proportion of the workers at the pottery were Irish and of Smith's build. In Stuart's statement before he died he never once said he had seen the face of either of his attackers. Miles Brown stated that he had passed the pottery at about 9.10pm and seen Smith talking to another man in hushed tones. When asked how he had recognised Smith, Dowling answered it was by his glazed hat. PC Allen gave testimony concerning the stains on Smith's clothing. He was asked if Smith had given the boot, stockings and breeches willingly or had he tried to hide them. PC Allen admitted that they had been given willingly. At the scene of the crime Allen had placed a piece of bloodstained cloth inside one of Smith's boots and it was suggested that the constable should have known better than to contaminate the boot. PC Allen was asked to produce the boot, stockings and stick and was asked if he could see any blood upon them. By this time the marks had faded so as to have almost disappeared. He admitted he could see none on the boot but could still see stains on the stick. Stuart had said that he had been hit with something made of iron, probably the kiln poker that had been found at the warehouse, but this discrepancy was overlooked. Another discrepancy in the evidence was the stockings. The stain was low down on the garment and it was pointed out that top boots would have covered this part of the material so how could they have become bloodstained if Smith had been wearing his boots when the attack took place.

A view overlooking the Tyne showing the Guildhall where the trial of Charles Smith was held in 1817. Author's collection

The trial judge ruled that there was a query as to whether the statement signed by Stuart could be used as evidence. One point was that it accused Smith of the robbery but not of murder. Stuart's state of mind was called into question because of the serious head and facial injuries he had sustained. Also, although Stuart's statement was read out to Smith, he was not present to hear the questions or answers given when the statement was written. Because of the concern revolving around Stuart's ability to identify his attacker the trial judge referred the case to twelve judges.

It was to be almost a year before the concerns were resolved and the trial re-opened. It took place at the Guildhall on 15 August 1817. At the end of the trial Smith was found guilty and sentenced to death. He seemed to accept his fate with quiet resignation and only asked that his body be given to his wife for burial.

Charles Smith, aged forty-nine, was hanged on Wednesday, 3 December 1817 on the Town Moor, a little north of the barracks on the opposite side of the road. Before his death, in a firm and impressive manner, he addressed the spectators at some length, denying having murdered Stuart and stating that he forgave all who had appeared against him. After joining in prayer with the Roman Catholic clergyman, Mr Worswick, Smith was launched into eternity. He had asked that his body be given to his wife for burial but his last wish was not granted as his body was taken to the Surgeons' Hall for dissection. It did not end there for Smith as some of his skin survived to be bound into a book about his trial and conviction. The macabre relic is now in the keeping of Newcastle City Library.

There was very little real evidence against Smith and if he was innocent, which is highly probable, his last year on earth must have been almost unbearable. He would have been locked up in Newgate Gaol with nothing but time to ponder on whether he would be allowed to live or if he would die with the hangman's noose around his neck. Smith would have also known that the guilty parties would never be caught as he had already been judged as the perpetrator of the crime.

CHAPTER 10

Matricide
1829

... more than 20,000 spectators gathered in the streets and around the gallows ...

Because of the fact that the perpetrator was a woman and the circumstances surrounding this whole sorry event from start to finish, the trial and subsequent execution of Jane Jameson was a well documented case of the period.

Jane was thirty and earned a meagre living by hawking fish and other commodities and as such was well-known in the town. She was also known as a habitual drunk and a disgusting creature of masculine appearance who wandered around in a semi naked state. Margaret Jameson, Jane's mother, lived at the Keelman's Hospital where rooms were set aside to accommodate the widows of keelmen. Jane visited her mother on a regular basis and one such visit was on Friday, 2 January 1829. Nine days later, on Sunday, 11 January, Margaret Jameson was pronounced dead. This resulted in Jane standing trial at the Moot Hall in Newcastle on Thursday, 5 March 1829 accused of matricide.

The first witness to be called at the trial was Mary Carr who lived three rooms away from Margaret's. On the day following New Year's Day, she had been on her way to the midden when she had heard shouting from Margaret's room. She had looked in through the open door as she passed. Mary stated that she saw Jane, very drunk, brandishing a poker in a threatening manner at Margaret. Mary went to the midden and as she returned Jane was at the door of Margaret's room shouting 'My mother, my mother'. Mary was frightened of Jane so scuttled back into her own room and shut the door.

That same day Ann Hutchinson had been visiting her mother who lived next door to Margaret. Called as the next

A sketch drawn of Jane Jameson at the time of her trial in 1829. Author's collection

witness, Ann stated that at about 2.30pm she had heard an argument take place between Jane and her mother. Jane had shouted 'You old, lousy, stane-naked, kill good man bitch'. Margaret had shouted back 'No, you whore! I did not kill my man but you killed your two bairns'. There was a scream and then total silence. The commotion had also attracted the attention of some of the other women who lived on the premises. Ann entered Margaret's room closely followed by

Fortuna Turnbull and Margaret Duncan. As they entered the room they noticed a poker lying in the middle of the floor. They then saw Margaret and realised that there was something wrong with her. The elderly woman was sitting on the floor like a rag doll with Jane trying to prop her up. The three neighbours lifted Margaret onto her bed and saw blood running down her left side that was seeping from a large wound in her breast. These events were corroborated by the other two women who had assisted Ann.

John Patterson, the beadle of the hospital, stated that he had asked Margaret who had done this to her and she had replied 'Jinny did it'. James Galbraith, the steward, said that Jane was not supposed to be on the premises because she was always in drink and troublesome. When Galbraith asked her that day what had happened Jane had said that Billy Elly had kicked Margaret with his shoe. Billy, or William Ellison, had been a friend of the family for about twelve years. Three of the other witnesses also said that Jane had accused Billy of the attack. It was established that Billy had not visited the hospital at all on that particular day.

Most of the witnesses agreed that Margaret was a quiet soul most of the time but was different when her daughter came to visit. Jane would bring her mother liquor and the two of them would get drunk and argue. They would both throw things and threaten one another. On the day in question both mother and daughter had been drinking.

During the days following the attack Jane had cared for her mother with the occasional help of a neighbour. On 5 January a doctor was called. He applied a poultice to the wound and suggested advice should be sought from the Newcastle Dispensary. Margaret told him that she had received the injury when she had fainted and fallen upon the poker. An assistant surgeon visited Margaret five days later and a principal surgeon on 11 January. By this time the wound had become inflamed and nothing could be done to save her life.

When Margaret's body was examined it was established that the wound had been caused by the poker and that it was probably hot at the time. Being hot, the poker would have cauterised the wound otherwise she would have probably bled to death immediately. The medical examiner said that considerable force had been used but he could not say, with any certainty, whether the poker had been thrust at Margaret or whether she had fallen upon it.

Jane denied naming Billy as the perpetrator and said she could not remember what had happened that fateful day as she had been asleep by the side of the fire. She accused one of the witnesses of only being at the court for the 5s (25p) a day she would receive.

After a trial lasting seven hours the judge summed up the proceedings by instructing the jury that they must decide whether Jane had struck the fatal blow. If they agreed that Jane was the perpetrator they must then consider whether this was murder or manslaughter. They were to disregard everything they had heard except the evidence within the court and decide whether Jane had meant to cause grievous bodily harm

The Keelmen's Hospital where Margaret Jameson lived and met her death at the hands of her daughter. Author's collection

in which case it was murder. If the jury came to the conclusion that Jane had no wicked intention then they must find her guilty only of manslaughter. The jury retired and in less than an hour they returned to give a verdict of guilty and sentence of death was pronounced. Jane sobbed as she was led from the dock.

On Saturday, 7 March the Reverend WA Shute, Reverend FA West, Wesleyan minister and Reverend R Green administered the sacrament. Jane was then pinioned and helped into a cart that transported her from the gaol in Carliol Square to the Town Moor. She was accompanied by Mr Turner, the turnkey, in order to support her but she sat firm all the way. In a macabre touch, the cart also held a coffin. Jane was the first to be taken to an execution from the new gaol. It was recorded that there were more than 20,000 spectators gathered in the streets and around the gallows to watch the procession and the final act. On horse-back in front of the cart was the town marshal, garbed in official dress; the town sergeants dressed in black with cocked hats and carrying swords and around it walked eight free porters with javelins and ten constables with staves. A mourning coach followed occupied by the Reverend R Green, Mr Scott, clerk of St Andrew's, Mr Adamson, under sheriff and Mr Sopwith, the gaoler. The large procession stopped at the gallows which had been erected a little to the north-west of the barracks.

After final prayers Jane stood on the platform of the cart. Two verses of *The Sinner's Lament* were sung by Mr Scott before a cap was placed over Jane's head and the noose around her neck. At exactly 10am the bell tolled from the tower of St Andrew's Church and Jane was heard to say 'I am ready' and in a few seconds, with barely any struggle, she was dead. After hanging for the required hour, Jane's body was taken to the Barber Surgeons' Hall where, with only the face exposed, it was displayed to the public for the rest of that day. Several thousand people were said to have filed through the foyer to view Jane's earthly remains. The body was then used by John Fife, a surgeon, for anatomical lectures to his students. This was to be the last time that the court ordered a criminal's body to be given to the surgeons.

The tower of St Andrew's Church from where the bell tolled at Jane Jameson's execution. It was customary to toll the bell for fifteen minutes before and after an execution. The author

The costs of the execution were recorded in the statement of the corporation and steward's accounts:

Expenses attending the execution of Jane Jameson	£. s. d.
To seven serjeants, 5s. each	1 15 0
To twenty constables, 3d. 6d. each	3 10 0
To sixteen free porters, 5s. each	4 0 0
To tolling St Andrew's great bell	0 2 6
To executioner	0 3 0
To cart and driver	0 15 0
To mourning coach	0 15 6
To nine horses for officers, 5s. each	2 5 0
To summoning twenty constables, 6d. each	0 10 0
To allowance for free porters, serjeants, constables &c	2 18 0
To a person attending the prisoner to the place of execution	0 5 0
To joiner's bill	8 5 3
To allowance to joiners	0 6 0
	£28 13 3

Here is a round sum for executing this poor creature. The 'joiner's bill' it must be understood, was for erecting the temporary gallows, making the coffin, &c, &c.

Jane was the first female to be hanged on the Town Moor since the execution of Alice Williamson on 7 August 1758.

CHAPTER 11

Murder in a Cellar
1844

*Her aunt was lying in a pool of blood and was
quite obviously dead ...*

Mark Sherwood and his wife, Ann, had lived in Peel
Street, Newcastle. At the same time the couple also
rented two rooms at Blandford Street. Early in 1844
the couple gave up their accommodation at Peel Street and
moved into the two underground, or cellar, rooms in
Blandford Street. The reason for them having rented two
properties at the same time became clear in March of that
year. Sherwood had been a soldier in the artillery and received
a small pension. It was thought that the couple lived on this
pension and whatever Ann could earn by selling work baskets
and other similar items but it later emerged that this was not
their only means of income. At the time of these events the
couple had been married about twelve years. Ann was fifty-two
and her husband some years older.

Sherwood was a heavy drinker and in March of 1844, just
after the couple had moved into Blandford Street, the
quarterly pension arrived. Sherwood disappeared for a few
days on his usual drinking spree. He returned home penniless,
so Ann, perhaps wanting rid of him for a little longer, pawned
some clothing for 5s (25p) and gave the money to him.

On 12 March Ann's niece, Ann Sutherland, called to see her
aunt. According to Sutherland's later testimony her aunt had
told her that Sherwood had returned after spending the pawn
money on drink and had threatened to do something to her
but he had made her swear on the bible not to say what the
threat was. At this point Sutherland said that her aunt had
dragged her hand across her throat in a gesture that she took
to mean that had been the threat. Sherwood was there at the

Looking across the Town Moor to Chimney Mills, probably the last view that Mark Sherwood saw before he was hanged in 1844. Author's collection

time and had gone on his knees to the niece and begged her to make peace between him and his wife. Sutherland left and went back to her home in Oakwellgate in Gateshead but said she was very worried about her aunt. She returned to Blandford Street around eight the following morning and was told by Sherwood, through a locked door who seemed sober, that his wife had gone to a neighbour's house and taken the key with her. This set alarm bells ringing as it was unusual for the door to be locked. Sutherland could do nothing but go home again and return to her aunt's rooms later. At about 11am the niece returned to Blandford Street but the door was still locked. There was no reply to her knocks and no sound from within, so Sutherland decided she needed to investigate. She went and borrowed a spare key that was held by John Ormiston who lived in the adjoining house.

The niece's suspicions that something was amiss were well founded. When she entered the cellar she was greeted by the sight of two bodies on the bare flags of the floor. Her aunt was lying in a pool of blood and was quite obviously dead as there was a gaping wound to her throat. Sherwood, although he appeared at first glance to be dead, was only in a drunken stupor. Sutherland alerted neighbours who in turn went for the police. Inspector Little of Westgate police station was quickly on the scene, followed by Dr Carr and Dr Taylor. Ann Sherwood's injuries were horrific. She had two deep gashes to her neck, which had almost decapitated her, two wounds to her lower jaw, a partially severed thumb and multiple cuts on her hands and arms. It was clear that many of the victim's injuries had been caused as she had tried to defend herself against a violent attack. The two doctors arrived at the conclusion that the murder had taken place at about 8 am, near to the time when Sherwood was telling Sutherland that his wife was visiting a neighbour.

Knowing there was nothing they could do for Ann the medical men attended to the still comatose Sherwood. They used a stomach pump to remove the alcohol but twice through the procedure the doctors thought that Sherwood was going to die. Eventually Dr White suggested using mustard blisters on Sherwood's hands and feet. Within a very short space of time they considered that Sherwood was out of danger. He was placed on a mattress in the corner of the kitchen and for the rest of the afternoon drifted in and out of sleep.

Meanwhile, Inspector Little had been looking about the two rooms. There was a dish of bloodied water in which it was thought Sherwood had washed his hands after he had committed the terrible deed. In the fire-grate were two razor blades and the outer door key was found hanging on a nail in the kitchen. In the second room Inspector Little found a still. Home-made whisky was being distilled which would have been far stronger than anything that could be bought over the counter. There were about thirty gallons in the fermenting stage, far too much for one person's use, so the conclusion was that an illicit business had been carried out. This explained why the couple had rented the extra rooms. The still and all the equipment with it were later removed by the excise men.

A post-mortem was carried out on Ann in which it was ascertained that the jugular vein, carotid artery and windpipe had been severed. She also had numerous other severe wounds about her hands, face and body. The conclusion was that the razor blades found in the grate had been used with considerable force to inflict the horrific injuries. Sherwood was charged with his wife's murder and the initial inquest was held at the *Grey Bull* public house which was immediately opposite the house where the murder had taken place. The outcome of the inquest was that Sherwood was committed for trial at the Summer Assizes before Chief Baron Pollock.

As there were no neighbours who were on familiar terms with the couple most of the testimony rested with Ann Sutherland, the niece. In her evidence she was very protective of her aunt. She stated that her aunt did not drink and would not have been involved in the illicit manufacture of whisky. The court had reservations on whether this was true or not as the still was in their lodgings so Ann must have, at the very least, condoned it. Sutherland denounced Sherwood as a drunken bully. As soon as he received his pension he would drink until it was spent. When under the influence of alcohol she described him as being violent and cruel and, although they had once been happy, the couple's marriage had deteriorated over the years. There was no doubt that Sherwood had murdered his wife as the couple had been the only occupants in rooms that were locked from the inside. It only rested with the jury to decide whether it was manslaughter or murder. If a person was under the influence of alcohol when a crime was committed it was often considered temporary insanity. The person may then be found not responsible for their actions as it would not be considered premeditated. Ann had died at about 8 am and at this time Sutherland stated that he was sober so the jury in this case felt that they had no other course but to return a verdict of guilty of wilful murder.

The night before his execution was to be carried out Sherwood made a full confession to the chaplain, Reverend L Paige. He said that on the night of 12 March he and his wife had been arguing before they had gone to bed. Ann had risen from their bed at some time through the night to attend to the distillery and had then returned to their bed and gone to sleep. She had woken early the following morning and lit the fire with Sherwood getting up at about 6 am. The argument of the previous night flared up again and Ann had been shouting at him. Sherwood lathered his face in preparation of shaving. As he took the razor from its case Ann's abuse of him became worse. He attacked her and after a struggle threw her to the floor and used the razor on her throat. Sherwood then disentangled himself from his wife's mangled body and threw the razors and case onto the fire. He stated he was perfectly sober at the time of the attack and it was afterwards that he drank a large amount of whisky and lapsed into unconsciousness on the floor. They had lived in the south before moving to Newcastle and at that time they had been happy with Ann content to sell work baskets. When they moved north Sherwood said it was Ann that organised the still. She had picked up her knowledge of the trade from an Irish

The Newcastle Barracks on the edge of the Town Moor. The first recorded gallows were situated near to this site. When these buildings were erected in 1806 the gallows were moved further north. Author's collection

family that she knew well. Sherwood said he had begged her to stop because if they were caught he would lose his pension. He stated that Ann Sutherland had lied in the courtroom. She had known about her aunt running the still and Sherwood had not seen his wife drag her hand across her throat nor had he begged Sutherland to make peace between himself and his wife. Sherwood added that he had not meant to hurt his wife and in no way was the murder premeditated.

Influential people of the town had a petition drawn up to try and get the sentence changed to transportation but this was unsuccessful. At midday on Friday 23 August Sherwood was led from his cell to step onto the carriage that waited to transport him on his final journey. Along Carliol and Northumberland Streets dense crowds packed the route. From every window with a view of the streets people were watching and waiting to catch a glimpse of the condemned man and his entourage on its way to the scaffold erected on the Town Moor racecourse. At just before 1pm Sherwood climbed the steps of the scaffold and stood with his head erect to await his fate. When the cap was about to be placed over Sherwood's head he asked that his eyes could remain uncovered. His request was granted and the executioner, John Murdoch, placed the rope around Sherwood's neck. As the prayers that were being chanted ended, the trap door opened and within seconds life was extinct.

This was the first use in Newcastle of the trap door known as 'the drop' so perhaps Sherwood had an easier death than his wife. He was the last person to be executed on the Town Moor. Sherwood was buried within the grounds of Newcastle Gaol.

Ann Sherwood's maiden name had been Grant and she had originally come from Wooler. She was buried in St John's churchyard.

CHAPTER 12

Patricide
1846

*Joicey's eyes were fixed on a book of prayers
which was opened in his hands.*

On Tuesday, 9 December Robert Joicey, who was fifty-seven, was found dead at his home at Cockle Park, Morpeth. It was obvious by his appearance that he had died in extreme agony. Joicey's wife, Isabella, his daughter, Margaret and his son, Ralph, lived with him. Ralph worked as a hind on a farm belonging to the Duke of Portland. Joicey's other son, William, lived at Hutton's Court in Pilgrim Street, Newcastle. On a post-mortem being carried out on Joicey's body by Dr Arthur Hedley of Felton and a surgeon, Robert Hawdon of Morpeth, it was determined that he had died from some form of poisoning. Although no trace of arsenic was found in the body, the symptoms that Joicey had exhibited before his death pointed to that being the poison used. The police were immediately alerted and Joicey's wife and daughter were arrested. On a search being made for Ralph, Police Constable Wigham found him at his brother's house and took him into custody.

At the initial inquest held at Morpeth George Pringle, an assistant at Mr Creighton's chemist shop in Morpeth, stated that a man, who may have been Ralph Joicey, had bought a quantity of poison about two months previously. The coroner instructed that Ralph, his mother and sister, should be taken to Morpeth Gaol to await trial. The date was set for 26 February 1846 at Newcastle Assizes before Justice Coleridge.

At the Assizes Ann Richardson was called as a witness. She had lived in as a servant to the Joicey family up until Martinmas. Ann stated that about two months before she left there was an argument which Robert Joicey had begun. He

Pilgrim Street Gate in about 1800. Ralph Joicey was arrested at his brother's house in Pilgrim Street for the murder of their father in 1846. Author's collection

had spoken 'very harshly' to his daughter and she had threatened her father saying he had better beware or she would poison him. Margaret Joicey denied that she had threatened her father but said that he was always calling her bad names. She had retaliated by telling him that he was making her think of the play *The Lass of Acklington* where the main character was accused of poisoning her father but was acquitted.

Dr Hedley gave evidence, saying that he had been treating Joicey for a minor ailment and on occasion he would leave powders for him at the *Portland Arms* public house to be collected by his family. The doctor added that on an occasion when he had been called to the house to treat Mrs Joicey she had shook her fist at her husband in anger at some remark he had made. One of the jurors was also a witness. He was a neighbour of the Joiceys and had been in their house one night recently but had left because of an argument that took place. The quarrel had been so intense he had been worried that they would do each other harm.

On the evening of 30 November there had been a knock at the door of the *Portland Arms*. Julia Coulson lived on the premises with her parents and it was she who answered the knock. Julia did not recognise the caller as he had been muffled up so his face was all but hidden and it was very dark. She assumed that the man was dressed that way because of the cold weather. In a low tone the bearer had said 'This is medicine for old Joicey' and handed Julia a parcel. The parcel was passed to a customer who said he was going to Cockle Park the following day. It was then given to Isabella Brown, the Joiceys' next door neighbour. She in turn gave it to Isabella Joicey.

Isabella Joicey could not read, so although she saw writing on the outer wrapper of the parcel, she did not know what the message was. Isabella gave it to her husband who opened it to find two lots of powders. The inscription on the outer paper was the instructions on the use of the contents and read:

I make you a present for Joicey. Take this large powder in a glass of ale or wine and the small one in a little honey or jelly, the one at night and the other in the morning.

Joicey took the large powder in a glass of gin and the couple went to bed. Through the night Isabella was woken by her husband saying he was going to be sick. Before he could leave the bed he began to vomit. The following morning Isabella gave her husband plenty of water to drink, thinking this would ease his discomfort. She threw the second powder on the fire as the first one had made him so ill. Joicey would not let his wife call the doctor in to see him but Ralph went to Dr Hedley and told him his father was vomiting. The doctor gave Ralph some powders for Joicey to take and the patient seemed to improve slightly. This remission did not last and by Sunday, 7 December Joicey had become seriously ill and Dr Hedley was called in to see him. When the doctor was told about the parcel he was baffled and said that he had left no medicines at the public house recently. Margaret Joicey gave the wrapping from the parcel with the message written upon it to Dr Hedley who later passed it on to the police. By the time of the doctor's visit Joicey was beyond medical help and he died the following evening.

Newgate Street, Morpeth in the nineteenth century. It was at his house in Cockle Park at Morpeth that Robert Joicey was murdered by his son. Author's collection

Ralph did not deny murdering his father. He said he had mixed a portion of arsenic in two lots of jalap (a form of laxative) and, disguising himself, had left them at the public house as if they were from Dr Hedley. It was his writing on the parcel wrapping. Ralph was asked why he had kept the arsenic so long before using it. His reply was that he did not know whether he could kill his father or not. He said the reason for the murder was because of the terrible way Robert Joicey had treated his family. It was suggested that Ralph could have just moved away but he said he would have been frightened to leave his mother and sister to the mercy of his father.

Margaret Joicey was arraigned on a charge of receiving, comforting and assisting to relieve her brother knowing that he had murdered their father. There was no evidence to support this charge and she was found not guilty.

Ralph was found guilty of the wilful murder of his father and, at the age of twenty-four, was hanged at a public execution at Morpeth on Wednesday, 18 March 1846. Snow had been falling all night and it was uncommonly cold for the time of year. The day had been declared a public holiday and, as there had not been an execution in Morpeth since 1822, when William Currie and Mark Lawson were executed, large crowds began to gather from six in the morning to witness the event, despite the bad weather. It was estimated that the number of spectators reached 900. As the procession, consisting of gaol governor, wardens, chaplain and the doomed man appeared the chattering amongst the crowds came to an abrupt halt. Joicey's eyes were fixed on a book of prayers which was opened in his hands. Only once did he look up and that was at the scaffold. Those near to him could see that his complexion was ashen and that he was trembling. As he stepped onto the scaffold the executioner was waiting. John Murdoch, by then seventy-six, had been employed to carry out the last sentence of the law on Joicey. Despite his age, Murdoch carried out the execution quickly and 'humanely' and it was all over within a matter of minutes. After death the body was left to hang for the customary hour and then taken down and interred within the confines of the gaol.

One newspaper report stated that many wept; others turned away their heads unable to bear the sickening sight. A conflicting report stated that the public houses were jammed with people singing and dancing and enjoying the holiday.

CHAPTER 13

The Railway Labourers
1847

*He had been fatally stabbed between the
thigh and abdomen.*

During the construction of the Newcastle and Berwick Railway contractors employed a mixture of Irish and English workers. Prejudice was rife and some of the workers did not labour together in perfect harmony. One argument that took place between Daniel Hives, an Englishman, and John Hugh Murray and George Matthews, who were Irish, had tragic consequences.

On Monday, 5 October 1846, after their shift had ended, Murray and Matthews had gone for a couple of drinks. They left the public house and walked along Benton Lane. William Oliver and Hives, who worked for Messrs Rush and Lawton, were driving waggons up the lane. Oliver was in front of Hives and on turning around he saw his companion's waggon go into a ditch. The two of them could not get the waggon out so Oliver went to fetch a horse. When he returned Murray and Matthews were running along the road. Hives was standing in the road with his face covered in blood. Oliver turned his horse and went after the two men with Hives running beside him. When they caught up the two attackers Murray turned and hit Oliver with a stick. Oliver decided the situation was serious and thought it prudent to get some assistance so rode off towards the railway embankment. He returned with three men but Hives and his attackers were no longer in the lane. By this time Hives was lying in the middle of a field dead from a stab wound. Murray and Matthews were caught and arrested. An initial inquest was held at Mr Boggin's *Black Bull* public house in Long Benton. The two men were then committed to stand trial at the Moot Hall before Baron Rolfe on 27 February 1847.

There had been two witnesses to the events that took place. One was Mrs Bryson who lived at Willington George Pit at Long Benton. She had been returning from Newcastle on Monday afternoon when she saw two men running along the coach road towards her. Another man was running after them wielding a stick. As the pursuer approached her Mrs Bryson saw that his face was covered in blood. She asked him what was happening and he replied that the two men he was chasing had beaten him up but the Irish would not get the better of an Englishman. He added that he would run until he dropped to catch them. Mrs Bryson ran to a nearby farm adjoining Benton Lane to get help. The farm belonged to Captain John Potts, a magistrate. Potts had already spotted the men and was standing watching from a stile at the bottom of the lane. He had heard one of the Irishmen threaten to murder their pursuer if he came too close. Mrs Bryson and Potts saw the three men climb a stile that led into Dog Kennel Field. Potts was worried about the outcome as the chaser had almost caught up with the chased so he followed them into the field. Suddenly the two Irishmen stopped to face their pursuer. Potts stepped between the men and tried to calm the situation but the Irishmen pushed him out of the way and lunged at the other man. There was a scuffle and then the Irishmen were off, one towards Byker's Hill and the other across the fields, and out of sight. Potts turned towards the man who had been attacked. He was standing looking down at his feet. Potts followed his gaze and saw blood trickling out of Hives' trouser leg. Then, in rapid succession, two large spurts of blood followed the trickle. Potts began to tell the injured man to sit down but before he could finish the sentence Hives swayed a little and then fell to the ground. He had been fatally stabbed between the thigh and the abdomen.

Potts's labourers were ploughing in a nearby field so he rounded them up to give chase to the two fugitives. Others joined in the search and the two men were soon caught.

Matthews tried to plead manslaughter and not murder. The reason for the altercation, he stated, began with a taunt from Hives when they passed him in the lane. Hives had shouted to them, 'Have you been paid off you Irish B———s?' Matthews

Map showing the location (circled) of Willington George Pit where Mrs Bryson lived. She was a witness to the murder of Daniel Hives in 1847. Reid's Handy Colliery Guide, 1898

insisted that he had not meant to kill but had used the knife only to disable Hives to prevent him from following them any further. Murray was acquitted but Matthews was found guilty of the murder of Daniel Hives and sentenced to death. In the time leading up to his execution Matthews spent the time with his spiritual advisor, the Reverend Mr Lowe of Morpeth. He was said to be deeply sorry for what he had done and had resigned himself to his punishment.

On the evening prior to the execution the scaffold, with its nine foot high beam, was erected in front of the main entrance to Morpeth Gaol by James Wallace of Newcastle.

At about 7 am on Wednesday, 17 March 1847 a body of police arrived from Newcastle to be stationed within the enclosure to prevent trouble should it arise. As this was to be a double execution (see Chapter 14) large crowds were expected to attend. As the time grew near about 3,000 people had gathered which was not as many as had been anticipated. At precisely 7.45am the bell began its melancholy toll. The two prisoners were escorted up the stairs of the scaffold by turnkeys where John Murdoch, the executioner, waited. The crowd went quiet and remained so until the double deed was over. The bell continued to ring for fifteen minutes and when it ceased the crowds dispersed to carry on with their daily business.

Daniel Hives had worked for Rush and Lawton for about three years and was well thought of. The media reported that after the murder his employers sacked all the Irish workers and refused to employ any man of that nationality again.

CHAPTER 14

The 'Proud' Father
1847

Hastily, the executioner took hold of Welch to stop him spinning and both men were drawn back up and dropped for the second time.

Thomas Proud worked as a hind to Mr Maughan of Newbrough Lodge, which was situated about five miles from Hexham. On 7 February Proud had his youngest child christened. After the christening the party went back to Proud's house and then to Mr Richard Surtees' public House at Newbrough where they each had two drinks. As Proud was leaving the public house a little later with his party they were accosted by James Welch. Welch was only twenty-two but had already earned himself a reputation of violence. He was known as a morose young man who had frequent outbursts of temper over trivialities. Welch had previously served four months in Morpeth Gaol for house-breaking near Wooler in 1842.

Welch had obviously had a bit to drink and became a nuisance to the group by taking hold of a girl who was with Robert Brown and asking her to go back into the public house and have a glass with him. The girl refused and neither she nor Brown was happy with the situation. Welch then took hold of another woman who was walking with Proud. He then fell, pulling the woman down with him. Proud told Welch to leave as he did not want his company upset. Welch continued to follow and once again grabbed the arm of the girl who was with Brown. When Brown objected Welch threatened to hit him. Proud stepped in between the two men and a short scuffle took place. Some of the guests managed to stop the fight and separate the men. Welch then took off his coat and, handing it to one of the guests, went for Proud. Blows were struck and Welch ended up on the ground. The party then carried on walking. Welch jumped up and, asking a young man to give him his walking stick, he once again followed Proud and his guests carrying the stick. As the party crossed the small bridge at the west of the village Welch caught up with them. By this time he was stripped to the waist and in a towering rage. He threw the stick towards the group and then approached Proud and struck at him twice. Proud put his hand to his face

Newcastle Gaol in 1825. James Welch was held here in 1847 until his trial for the murder of Thomas Proud. Author's collection

and stepped back a few paces before falling to the ground. He had a deep wound from just under his left ear to the middle of his chin and from this blood was gushing in a torrent. There was also a nasty cut on Proud's left wrist from him lifting his arm to protect himself from Welch. His friends carried him to a barn near to his house but he had died within seconds of the attack. Welch ran off but was arrested later at a public house at Fourstones by PC George Ridley. The knife that Welch had used was found in the middle of the road near Fourstones station.

At the initial inquest the jury were taken to where the attack had taken place to view the blood stains on the ground. They then proceeded to the barn where the body was lying. The sight would have turned the strongest stomach as the knife had cut the arteries and the body was saturated with blood.

Welch was committed to stand trial at the Moot Hall before Baron Rolfe on 26 February. There was no doubt that Welch had killed Proud. The knife that was found belonged to Welch and was covered in blood. He also had blood on his chest and his hands when he was arrested and there had been witnesses to the whole sorry affair. The only thing to be decided by the jury was whether this had been manslaughter in self defence or murder. Even though Proud had fought with Welch and knocked him down, at the time of the knife attack the victim had been walking away so it could not be deemed self defence. Welch was said to have sobbed throughout his trial. The jury found him guilty of Proud's murder and sentence of death was passed.

After the trial it was reported that Welch assumed his usual arrogant demeanour and displayed no remorse for his actions. He wrote to his friends asking that they visit him but they declined. Their reply was that while they were sorry for the situation he was in, due to the horrid nature of his crime they felt they had to deny his request. Perhaps this made a difference to his attitude or perhaps it was the persistence of the Reverend Finch who went to his cell every day to try and talk Welch into making his peace with God. Whatever the reason the day before the execution was to take place Welch took the sacrament and begged for exoneration for his sins.

Welch had been working as a labourer at Prudholm Quarry. The quarry was near the scene of the brutal murder of 'Joe the Quilter' which had taken place a few years previously. The murderer had never been caught and the media made mention of Welch perhaps being connected with the crime. This suggestion was never elaborated upon and was perhaps only 'media frenzy'. Whether he was guilty of one murder or two, Welch suffered the extreme penalty of the law when he was executed by John Murdoch, who was seventy-nine, on Wednesday 17 March, alongside George Matthews (see Chapter 13) in a double execution.

As the final Amens of the prayer were heard the drop fell but the executioner had miscalculated the length of rope used leaving it too long. Instead of the relatively quick death that everyone present expected the feet of the two men were heard to touch the fallen drop. It could be seen by all that the two men were suffering extreme agony. Matthews' body was quivering and twitching while Welch's lips were moving, probably begging for release from his pain, as his body was spinning around and around. Hastily, the executioner took hold of Welch to stop him spinning and both men were drawn back up and dropped for the second time. Most of the crowd were so disgusted by the sickening spectacle that they dispersed immediately. Hawkers went round the few stragglers that remained selling the 'last dying speech and confession' of Matthews and Welch. Both bodies were buried within the grounds of the gaol. This was the last public execution to be held at Morpeth.

CHAPTER 15

He Never Meant to Hurt Her
1850

He was trembling and those nearest him could hear him praying.

Patrick Forbes lived with his wife, Elizabeth, who was thirty-eight, and their four children, Bridget, who was grown, Thomas, who was fifteen and a boy and a girl of seven and four. They occupied two rooms on the top floor of a house at Clogger's Entry at the head of the Side. The house was one of the many large buildings in Newcastle that were rented off in rooms to poorer families. The family were Irish and Forbes, who was forty, worked as a labourer. He was known as being a violent and quarrelsome man having been arrested on four occasions for being drunk and disorderly and once for an assault on his wife.

Forbes and his wife had spent the early afternoon of Friday, 29 March drinking at *Robertson's* spirit shop and returned home at about 4 pm. Elizabeth entered the house first and lay down at the bottom of the stairs in a drunken stupor. Forbes then staggered in and tried to wake his wife. He was unsuccessful so decided to carry her up the stairs to their rooms. Margaret Dees, who lived at the top of the first flight of stairs, had been looking after the two young Forbes' children. Forbes called her to give him a hand to get Elizabeth onto his back. Carrying his wife piggy-back fashion Forbes managed the first lot of stairs but dropped his wife at Margaret's door. He then took hold of his wife under the shoulders and Margaret took her feet and, carrying her in that fashion, they made it to the top landing. Forbes took the room key from his wife's pocket and inserted it in the lock but could not get the door to open. Margaret went back down to her room and returned with a poker with which Forbes forced an entry. By this time another neighbour, Mrs Wheatley, had heard the commotion and was on the landing. The two women lifted Elizabeth and laid her on her bed.

Bridget and her father had had a row and he had thrown her out three days previously. She had returned that afternoon just in time to witness her mother being carried upstairs. Bridget sneaked up behind them and peeked through the hole in the door that Forbes had made with the poker. She watched the two women lay her mother on the bed. Her father was on the floor vomiting. Bridget stood back for a few minutes and then looked again. By this time her father was lying on the floor seemingly asleep. Mrs Wheatley woke him and asked him to lend her sixpence (2.5p). Forbes roused himself but made no reply. Bridget stepped back as the women left the room and went downstairs. She waited a few more minutes and then entered the room. Her mother was lying on top of the bed fully dressed and her father was in bed partly undressed. They both appeared to be fast asleep. Bridget noticed as she was leaving the room that the fire in the grate was dying out. She then went downstairs to Margaret's room where her young brother and sister were.

It is doubtful whether the two younger children had been fed that day and Bridget went back to her parents' room at about 8 pm to get them some bread. It was quite dark by this time and although she heard snoring could not tell who it was. Afterwards she said she thought the fire had gone out. Later, at about 10 pm, Bridget went back to the room for bread for the children's supper. Margaret went with her holding a candle but did not enter the room. Bridget glanced over at the bed but could not see much in the darkness. The two youngest children and Bridget were still in Margaret's room at about 1am the following morning when they heard three or four muffled cries. Shortly after this Thomas Forbes came and asked Margaret for a candle saying that he thought his mother was dead. Not bothering with a candle, Margaret and Bridget ran upstairs. Bridget stood at the door while Margaret entered the room. Forbes was sitting on the edge of the bed, dressed only in his shirt, rocking to and fro and crying. There was a now a fire in the grate so Margaret lit a piece of paper and lent

Entrance to the Side where Patrick Forbes and his family lived in 1850. Author's collection

over the bed. From the door Bridget could see her mother on top of the bed clothes. She was going to have a closer look but her father came over and shut the door on her. Bridget ran downstairs and out of the house to go and fetch her uncle who lived nearby.

PC William Lauderdale was on duty that night and saw Bridget run from the house crying, so he immediately went to investigate. Margaret was on the landing and when the constable asked what was wrong she told him that Elizabeth Forbes was dead. When PC Lauderdale entered the room the first thing he saw was a large smear of blood on the floor with a handprint on it. Elizabeth was lying on the bed on her back. She was partially dressed but her legs were bare and bloodstained. The bedding beneath her legs was saturated with blood and resembled the floor of a slaughter-house. A handkerchief was crumpled up beside the bed and looked as though it had been used to mop up some of the blood. The constable checked Elizabeth to see if there was any sign of life but although her body was still warm she was not breathing. Forbes was sitting in the room still only half dressed. There was blood on his shirt and his hands. A surgeon was sent for and Dr Rayne attended at about 2 am. Because of the heat in the room from the fire he could not be sure how long

A sketch shown to the jury of the rooms in Clogger's Entry where Patrick Forbes murdered his wife. Author's collection

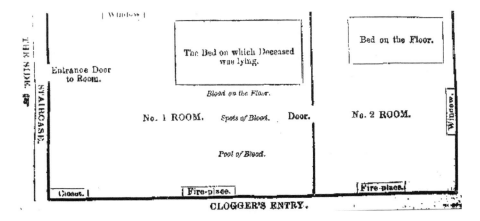

Elizabeth had been dead but thought it was probably an hour or so. Elizabeth's chemise, petticoat and another piece of cloth were lying on her abdomen. The blood on her legs was smeared as if they had been wiped. That she had been murdered the doctor had no doubt but could find no external wounds to the body to explain how she had died. PC Lauderdale had sent for a colleague, PC John Weddell, and the two of them searched the rooms to see if they could find any sort of weapon. They found tools, including knives and screwdrivers, which Forbes would have used in his line of work, but none of these had anything resembling blood on them. There was also a poker half in and half out of the fire. When the search was complete Forbes was arrested and charged with the murder of his wife. The initial inquest was held at Mr Sayer's *Blue Bells Inn* on the Side.

Dr Rayne had performed a post-mortem on Elizabeth's body and his findings were almost beyond belief. At the inquest and the following trial he demonstrated his findings by drawings and the use of a skeleton. Some form of sharp instrument had been inserted between Elizabeth's legs to a depth of about ten or twelve inches and moved about. All the internal parts that the weapon had come into contact with had been ripped and mutilated. In Dr Rayne's opinion Elizabeth could have taken up to twenty minutes to bleed to death and her agony would have been indescribable. She would have probably, even in her drunken state, been able to scream initially. In surgical operations it had been found on many occasions that when a person's abdomen was cut a loss of voice nearly always ensued. The doctor thought it impossible that Elizabeth could have inflicted these wounds upon herself because of the angle in which the implement had entered and the extreme pain it would have caused.

The time of death that the doctor had estimated at 1am fitted in with the cries Bridget heard and also with Thomas Forbes's testimony. Thomas was employed by Mr Hutchinson, a tallow chandler, and had come home from work sometime after 5 pm on Friday to find his parents asleep in bed and obviously drunk. He had gone back out and returned at about 10 pm when he had gone straight to bed in the next room to his parents. At about 1 am his father had woken him and told him his mother was dead and that was when he had gone to get a candle from and fetch Margaret Dees. After all the evidence was heard Forbes was committed to stand trial at the following Assizes.

At the trial, on 31 July, at the Moot Hall before Justice Wightman, the evidence was pieced together to give a picture of what had happened at Clogger's Entry. It was thought that Forbes had woken through the night and for reasons known only to him had used the poker to inflict fatal injuries on his wife. He had relit the fire and placed the poker in it to destroy any bloodstains that were on it and then tried to wipe the blood from his wife's legs.

The judge summed up the case by saying that there was no doubt as to the manner of Elizabeth's death and that she had been murdered. A verdict of manslaughter could only be brought when an argument took place and a death resulted through the heat of the moment by the infliction of a blow or a stab wound. In this particular case the manner of death was brutal and premeditated. The perpetrator had also tried to be cunning and dispose of evidence of the crime. Forbes may have been under the influence of alcohol but he was not so drunk that he was unable to carry his wife up the stairs and break his door open. He was also quite coherent when PC Lauderdale entered the premises. Forbes had the reputation of being a violent and thoroughly unpleasant man and it was known that he had assaulted his wife on previous occasions. The verdict could only be guilty of wilful murder but the jury must decide whether it was Forbes or someone else that committed the act.

The jury retired and were only absent for a few minutes. When the judge asked for their decision the reply from the foreman was:

We find that the deceased, Elizabeth Forbes, died from the most violent and brutal injuries, maliciously inflicted by her husband, Patrick Forbes, and we therefore find a verdict of guilty of wilful murder against Patrick Forbes.

Justice Wightman, after a closing speech, passed sentence of death upon Forbes with no hope of a recommendation for

Another view of the Side where families were crowded together into rooms in large old buildings. Author's collection

mercy. As Forbes was led from the court his children were standing in the entrance room of the Moot Hall in the custody of several policemen. The two younger children tried to spring forward to reach their father and it was with difficulty the police held them back. Their heart rending cries upset all who were within hearing. Bridget, who was described as a personable young woman, was wringing her hands and weeping uncontrollably.

Before the sentence was carried out Forbes made a declaration before Alderman George Dunn and Mr Thomas, the Governor of the gaol, in which he declared that he loved his wife sincerely and never meant to hurt her. He was drunk and could remember nothing about that night. He realised he must have perpetrated the deed as there was no one else there and that he deserved to hang under the laws of the country.

Forbes was to be executed on Saturday, 24 August at 8 am. Wooden barriers were erected across Carliol Street and around Carliol Square and police were in attendance as a temporary gallows was erected on the north boundary wall of the gaol. On Friday the *Newcastle Arms* had been full and the landlord had sold window seats to the customers who could afford to pay. Throughout the night crowds had begun to gather around the vicinity of the gallows. It was later reported that the onlookers numbered 16,000, more than half of whom were women and the majority of the lower classes. Amongst the crowd were the four Forbes' children. The executioner, seventy-four-year-old Nathaniel Howard, had visited the gallows several times as it was being erected and was jeered and hissed at by the spectators.

As the time drew near and Forbes appeared the clamour ceased. He was trembling and those nearest him could hear him praying. When he was told to step forward he was unable to do so and had to be lifted onto the drop. Howard placed the hood over Forbes' head, the noose around his neck and gave the signal for the bolt to be withdrawn, but, instead of falling straight down through the drop Forbes fell partially on and partially off the scaffold. He was hoisted up and dropped again with great speed to meet his death on the second attempt. His body was buried within the confines of Newcastle Gaol.

CHAPTER 16

The West Walls
1863

Elements in the crowd began to lay bets as to whether Vass would beg for mercy or go to his fate with resignation.

The New Year is supposed to herald hope and new beginnings. Not so for fifty-year old Margaret Docherty on New Year's Day, 1863. Margaret Kennedy had married John Docherty in 1832 in Glasgow and later the couple moved to Newcastle to live in Buckingham Street. To celebrate the New Year Margaret and her husband had spent the day drinking and ended up at *Ireland's* public house in Gallowgate. Docherty had had enough to drink by this time and tried to get his wife to go home with him. She refused so her husband pulled her out of the bar. When they got outside there were three men standing on the footpath. One of the men hit Docherty, knocking him to the ground. Docherty did not want further trouble so made his way home thinking his wife was close behind him. The following morning he was awoken by the police and taken to the mortuary. He was shown an apron that was soaked with blood, a cap and a pair of shoes which Docherty recognised as the garments Margaret had been wearing the previous day. The police told him that Margaret's body had been found at the West Walls.

Two men had gone to the Westgate police station to report finding the body. When the police attended the scene they were sickened by what they found. Margaret's shoes, cap and stockings were found a good distance from where she had died. There was mud on the soles of her feet where she had been walking barefoot. Margaret's dress had been almost ripped from her body and she was covered in grime. Dirt on the lower parts of her knees seemed to indicate that she had

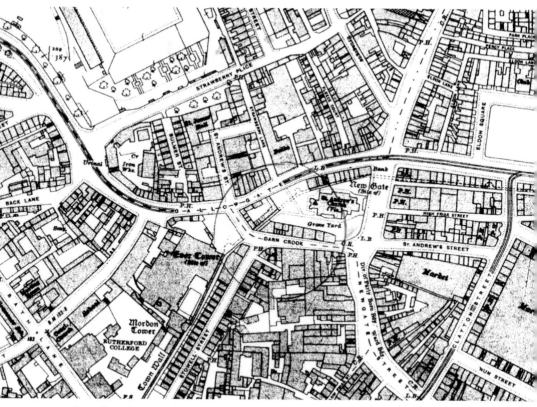

A portion of a map showing the location of Darn Crook. George Vass dragged Margaret Docherty up this lane before he brutally raped and murdered her.
Ordnance Survey, Newcastle, 1914

been kneeling on the ground at some point. Her face had been completely disfigured, with the nose smashed to a pulp. The right hip, inner thigh and the area above the pubic bone were scratched and bruised and deep wounds had been inflicted. A medical examination of the body was carried out by Dr Rayne. His findings were that the injuries had been inflicted using elbows, feet and a knife. Margaret had been brutally raped before she was murdered and the doctor stated that he had never seen such injuries on a human being except in accidents caused by a machine.

Witnesses that had been in the area at the time came forward to relate what they had seen and the name of George

The West Walls as they would have looked at the time of the rape and murder of Margaret Docherty. Author's collection

Vass appeared in numerous statements as having been recognised as the man dragging a woman up Darn Crook by her hair. Three men, Buckham, Nesbitt and Gillespie, stated that the woman looked very drunk. They had seen Vass throw her to the ground and rape her. Although the woman was screaming the three men decided it was none of their business and went on their way without interfering.

Vass was nineteen and lived in Stowell Street with his father, a cab driver. Once the police had made their enquiries and listened to what the witnesses had to say they went to Stowell Street to talk to Vass. His clothes were found to be bloodstained and when his pockets were searched he was found to have a knife in his possession. Vass was arrested and charged with murder.

At his trial his defence, Mr Blackwell, argued that although Vass had committed rape, Margaret was alive when he left her. The prosecution suggested that, after the three witnesses had left, Vass continued the violent attack and, after he had raped Margaret he then had proceeded to kick and stab his defenceless victim to death. The jury believed the prosecution and Vass was found guilty.

George Vass was hanged on Saturday, 14 March by Thomas Askern. His execution took place on top of the wall at Newcastle Gaol facing the steps of the Royal Arcade. After it was ascertained that he was dead, his body was left to hang for the customary hour and then buried within the confines of the gaol.

News reports of the day stated that there were more than 5,000 people, the most lawless and disreputable of the community, gathered to witness the spectacle. The crowd held possession of Carliol Square but a strong barrier had been erected to keep a walkway clear around the walls of the gaol. Elements in the crowd began to lay bets as to whether Vass would beg for mercy or go to his fate with resignation. As the time of the execution drew near the crowd swelled. The early arrivals had managed to obtain a place near to the barriers with the best view. As the crowd grew and became more compact many of those nearest to the barriers fainted under the crush of bodies. The spectacle of a man twitching in his

The West Walls as they look today. The author

last moments at the end of a rope was too much for some as, when the drop fell, several of the women in the crowd screamed and there was a rush of many to get away from the awful sight. A riot broke out and people were pushed to the ground and trampled on. The cries of the injured added to the terrible scene of confusion. This was to be the last time there would be such a battling, swearing mob turning out to watch an execution at Newcastle as Vass was the last man to be hanged there publicly.

CHAPTER 17

At the End of the Day
1875

... with a final jerk, Anderson was no longer of this world.

John William Anderson, who was thirty-two, lived with his wife, Elizabeth, aged twenty-nine, and one six-year-old son, at Mitford Street in Newcastle. The couple had another boy, who was nine, who lived with Anderson's mother in London. Anderson had been a private in the 98th Regiment but had been 'bought out' by his wife. He had then held a position as a clerk for a short time before moving to Mitford Street. The premises, besides living accommodation, provided a meagre living for the couple from a small provisions shop. It was generally known among their friends and neighbours that the couple had not been getting on well together for the previous two years as they had often been heard quarrelling.

On Saturday, 28 August Anderson, his wife and son, visited a neighbour. The couple had a few drinks and appeared to be on good terms while they were out. Elizabeth said she had to go and pull the shop shutters down and her husband offered to go with her to help. They arrived home at about 9.30 in the evening but their friendly mood must have changed because they began to argue. The door of the provisions shop was in two halves and Anderson shut the lower part leaving his son on the other side of the door. According to the young boy, when Anderson refused to open the door to let him in Elizabeth shouted that he was not to lock the boy out. Anderson had then opened the door and approached his son in a threatening manner. The boy began to cry and backed away. Anderson then shut the door again still leaving his son outside. Elizabeth tried to get to the door to unlock it but

Anderson blocked her from doing so. Elizabeth had then picked up a large bacon knife and approached her husband with it. Anderson managed to wrest the knife from his wife's grasp and she ran behind the counter. The boy then saw his father follow his mother and strike at her with the knife again and again. The piercing screams that rang out both frightened the boy away from the door and at the same time attracted the attention of people in the vicinity.

Sarah Dodds and Ralph Taylor, who both lived in Tyneside Terrace, rushed to the shop. As they tried the door they found both halves were locked. Then the bottom half opened and Anderson stooped down and came out. Sarah grabbed his collar and asked him what he had done. Anderson replied that 'he had done for her'. When the neighbours entered the shop it was in darkness so a candle was brought. In the dim light Taylor saw a bloodstained knife on the floor in front of the counter and Elizabeth lying nearby. Kit Danskin's kitchen backed on to the Anderson's shop and she had heard the commotion. When everything went quiet she also entered the shop. Kit cradled Elizabeth's head until the doctor arrived.

Anderson had made his way straight to the nearby Laurel Street police station. There he told Sergeant Kennedy and PC Dixon that he had stabbed his wife to death. The two police officers placed Anderson in custody and went to Mitford Street. Hoping Elizabeth may still be alive, PC Dixon returned to the police station and sent for Dr May of Scotswood Road to attend. The doctor arrived very quickly but Elizabeth was already beyond help. She had sustained a wound under the left arm, one of her ribs was divided, four back wounds in which the knife had penetrated through to the heart and two flesh wounds. In all but the flesh wounds the knife had been driven in with considerable force. Anderson also had a deep cut across the palm of his hand which he said he had received in self defence by grabbing the blade of the knife when he took it from his wife. When Dr May could do no more for Elizabeth he went to the police station and stitched Anderson's wound.

An initial inquest was held at the *Durham Ox Inn* before the coroner, JT Hoyle. Elizabeth's father, Ashley Walker, gave testimony to the fact that Anderson was a man of intemperate habits who had mistreated his wife throughout their marriage. Walker stated that his daughter did not drink but this was refuted by other witnesses. The neighbours who had attended the scene immediately after the stabbing also gave evidence as to what they had seen and heard. A verdict of wilful murder was returned and Anderson was committed to stand trial at the following Assizes.

The trial took place at the Newcastle Winter Assizes on 1 December before Justice Denham. The jury found Anderson guilty but with a strong recommendation for mercy. Petitions for clemency were sent to the Home Secretary along with the

A portion of a map showing the location of Mitford Street. It was here that John Anderson murdered his wife in 1875. Ordnance Survey, Newcastle and Gateshead 1894

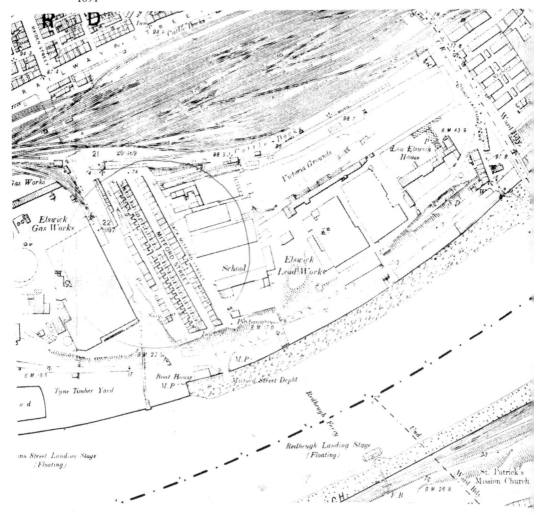

jury's recommendation but these were denied and the date for the execution was set for Thursday, 23 December.

The scaffold was the same as the one used for George Vass twelve years previously. The only difference was the position in which it was erected. For the execution of Vass the scaffold was elevated so that the final moments of his life could be witnessed by the public. For Anderson the scaffold was erected nearly level with the ground so it was hidden from anyone other than the few whose attendance was compulsory.

The morning of the execution dawned cold and grey. The gaol was eerily silent with nothing to hint at the gruesome drama that was to take place until the bell began to toll at 7.45 am. William Marwood, the executioner, had arrived the previous day and slept at the gaol. In the doorways of some of the houses opposite a few of the occupiers stood in silence. Small clusters of three to a dozen people began to gather from the foot of the Arcade stairs to Erick Street. In sharp contrast to the shouting, uncontrollable mob of twelve years before, these people talked in little more than whispers. A small group of men and boys were on the roof of Mr Mastaglio's house opposite the gaol. They were stood on the coping at the very corner of the building trying to peer over the wall.

Just before 8 am Marwood entered the cell in which Anderson was being held. The only sound was the voice of the Chaplain, Reverend Bowland, praying. Marwood placed the pinioning straps on Anderson. The Governor of the gaol then entered with two warders and told Anderson it was time. The small party then walked towards the scaffold to the sound of the church bell tolling and the Chaplain's muted tones. Anderson never flinched and placed himself directly over the drop without any assistance. Marwood quickly pinioned the condemned man's legs and placed the white cap over his head. Marwood bent down to the lever and the black flooring opened. There was a thud as the rope stiffened and, with a final jerk, Anderson was no longer of this world. He was buried in the north-east corner of the gaol.

CHAPTER 18

An Unhappy Marriage
1875

Charlton had shot himself in the cheek and the bullet was lodged in his head.

Richard Charlton was a labourer working for William Robson on a large farm at Gardner's Houses on the outskirts of Dinnington. He met Sarah Duxfield Fenwick at a barn dance held at Dinnington. She was the sister of his employer's wife and, after a short courtship, the couple decided to get married. On her father's death Sarah had been left £300, which was a large sum of money at that time. All Sarah's relatives thought that Charlton was only after her money and tried to talk her out of the marriage. Sarah was having none of it, she was in love and on 12 May 1873 the couple married in secret. They lived at Horton Grange for a short while and then moved back to Dinnington. Charlton took up employment as a labourer for Mr Taylor at a farm two miles from Dinnington. The couple had only been married a short time when arguments began over Sarah's inheritance. It seems that Charlton wanted some of it spent but she wanted it left in the bank. Sarah then found she was pregnant and the situation became much worse. Charlton apparently became very cruel to his wife. Arrangements had been made for her to have her child at Gardner's Houses Farm so that her sister, Ann, could look after her. On 7 April 1875 Sarah gave birth to a boy. Charlton came to see his son and the couple argued over a name for him. Ann joined in the argument and Charlton threatened to hit her saying that she was trying to turn his wife against him. Because the marriage had become so unhappy Sarah decided not to return to Charlton but to stay with her sister. Charlton visited the farm on numerous occasions begging Sarah to return home with him but she refused.

Very early on the morning of 5 June Charlton called at the farm and was told that Sarah was not awake yet. He left and returned that afternoon. Sarah was just entering the kitchen as her husband came in the back door. Once again Charlton asked her to go home with him and once again Sarah refused. Ann, another sister, Margaret Bennett and a friend, Jane Robinson, were in the parlour when they heard angry voices coming from the kitchen. They went to investigate with Ann entering the kitchen first. When she saw Charlton arguing with his wife she told Sarah to open the door and see Charlton out. He started shouting at Ann accusing her of causing mischief. Once again Ann calmly told Sarah to see Charlton out. As Sarah went to open the door Charlton grabbed her arm, pulled a revolver from his pocket and fired twice at Sarah's head and then turned the weapon on Ann and fired once. She felt the bullet graze her cheek and in fear of her life turned and ran. Jane was holding Sarah's baby and she also ran and found a hiding place outside. Ann ran into the pantry where Margaret was crouched, terrified, in a corner. The last time the three women had seen Sarah she was lying on the floor moaning in

Newcastle Infirmary in 1855. It was here that Richard Charlton was taken for treatment after he murdered his wife and then tried to kill himself in 1875. Author's collection

agony. Charlton had followed Ann and fired the revolver again, this time the bullet hit Margaret. In a strength born of fear Ann pushed the pantry door closed and held it. Charlton tried to open it but could not. He then started firing at the door but the bullets did not penetrate the thick wood. Enraged, Charlton rushed at the door again, this time succeeding in partially opening it. Ann revealed part of her hand through the opening when she attempted to push the door shut again. Charlton fired and sliced through her thumb and the top of her hand. He then went outside and tried to fire in through the pantry window but missed his aim. Ann heard him re-enter the house, then one shot, then complete silence. How long Ann stayed motionless in the pantry she did not know but the eerie silence continued for what must have seemed like an eternity. Eventually, summing up all the courage she could muster, Ann opened the door and crept out of her refuge. Charlton was lying motionless on the floor beside Sarah.

Bartholomew Watson, one of the farm labourers, had heard the last shot and had sent for assistance. He entered the house

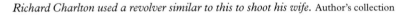

Richard Charlton used a revolver similar to this to shoot his wife. Author's collection

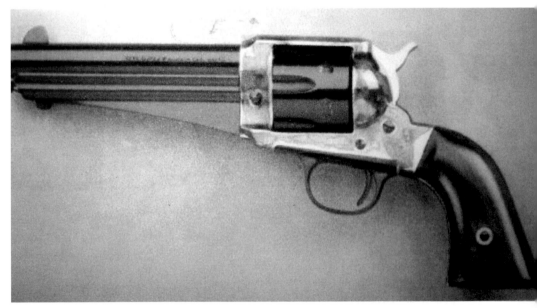

at the same time Jane came out of hiding, still holding Sarah's son. Between them they lifted Sarah onto the sofa. They then brought a mattress into the kitchen and lifted Charlton onto it. The police and two doctors were soon on the scene. Dr Jamieson and Dr Heath did not think that Charlton would survive a journey to the Newcastle Infirmary so had him transported to his own house under police guard. Charlton had shot himself through the cheek and the bullet was lodged in his head. Ann's injuries to her face and hands were serious but not life threatening. Sarah died the following day and Margaret died later.

Charlton survived but was completely paralysed down his left side. He was not recovered sufficiently to be tried at the Summer Assizes but eventually recovered enough to stand trial on 2 December. His defence put in a plea of insanity due to extreme provocation. It was determined that Charlton had purchased the five chamber revolver from a pawn shop a few days prior to the murder. It was also pointed out that he had reloaded the revolver during the attack. The verdict was that the whole event had been calculated and premeditated.

There was a strong feeling of sympathy for the condemned man as it was felt that he had been provoked by Sarah leaving him and keeping his child from him. A petition with numerous signatures was sent to the Home Secretary asking for a reprieve. The grounds put forward for the request were that Charlton had been treated badly by his wife and her relatives and it was this treatment that had provoked him into committing the rash acts. There was also the fact that he was now feeble and paralysed and it did not seem moral to execute a man so badly maimed. The request was denied and Richard Charlton, aged twenty-eight, was hanged at Morpeth on Thursday, 23 December 1875 by William Marwood.

This was the first private execution to take place at Morpeth and the authorities were faced with the problem of finding an area that was hidden from the public and the other prisoners. When the gaol was built it was not foreseen that executions would ever be anything but public. Eventually the scaffold was erected near to the south-west wall. Another diversion from previous executions was the absence of the sound of the church bell. This was usually tolled for fifteen minutes before and after the event. The council agreed at a meeting that the bell should stay silent because of the early hour and the shock to the community.

There was about £240 of Sarah's money in a bank account and Charlton had £10 in money and some furniture. Charlton's brother, Joseph, agreed to take care of the orphaned child and the money would go towards the child's care.

CHAPTER 19

Capers in the Snow
1876

Schooler and Arnott ran back ... to find Wood lying on the footpath with his chest and the snow around him red with blood.

George Hunter, William Wood, Robert Schooler and Thomas Arnott were pitmen in local collieries around Dinnington. On 9 December 1875 they decided to go out for an afternoon's shooting. Except for Wood all the men were carrying a gun. By about 5.30pm darkness began to fall so Wood, Hunter and Arnott decided to go for a few jars of ale in the *Carrgate Inn* at the lower end of Dinnington. Schooler was not a drinker so went to see a friend after arranging to meet up with his companions later on that night. The three men spent a pleasant evening at the inn and left at about 10 pm when Schooler returned. Another two men, Sampson Mead and Thomas Thorn, left with them. Hunter, Schooler and Arnott had their guns slung over their shoulders as they headed towards Dinnington Church. The ground was covered with soft white snow and Wood began throwing snowballs at Mead. It was just a bit of fun and was taken as such. Mead and Thorn came to where they lived so the other four said goodnight and carried on walking. Schooler and Arnott were some little distance in front of the other two when Wood began throwing snowballs again, this time at Hunter. Hunter was not amused at all and shouted to Wood that if he carried on he would shoot him. Wood, not for a minute taking him seriously, just laughed and continued throwing snowballs. Suddenly a shot rang out causing Schooler and Arnott to stop in their tracks. Hunter casually strolled up to them and asked for a powder flask. Schooler and Arnott asked if he had fired the gun and Hunter answered that

Dinnington Colliery where Wood, Hunter, Schooler and Arnott worked in 1875.
Author's collection

he had. There was no sign of Wood so, partially in jest, they asked if the shot had hit their friend. Hunter once again answered in the affirmative. Schooler and Arnott ran back the way they had come to find Wood lying on the footpath with his chest and the snow around him red with blood. Hunter was still standing where they had left him holding his gun when the police and a doctor arrived. Dr Walker pronounced Wood dead adding that death would have been almost instantaneous. When Constable Davidson arrested Hunter he seemed confused and had to be almost dragged along the road.

Hunter was committed for trial before Baron Bramwell. With the clear evidence of the two witnesses the whole trial lasted less than an hour. Hunter was found guilty with a recommendation for mercy. The recommendation was forwarded to the Home Secretary but was denied. This had been a cold-blooded murder over a triviality.

Twenty-three-year-old Hunter was hanged by William Marwood at Morpeth on Thursday, 28 March 1876. He was interred within the grounds of the gaol with the coffin end to end with that of Richard Charlton who had been executed the previous year.

This was the last execution to take place at Morpeth.

Chapter 20

A Shooting at Walker-on-Tyne 1886

He met his doom with a crucifix held firmly in his hands and a prayer on his lips.

Patrick Judge had lived with his wife, Jane, in a not too happy marriage, at Walker-on-Tyne. The couple had a small shop selling fish and other food provisions. They would both hawk their wares in the neighbouring villages from a horse and cart. Judge had served as a soldier in the 88th Foot from 1859 until 1870 with most of that time spent in India. After his discharge he took employment as a labourer at Byker. Whilst working there Judge was involved in an accident as a result of which he had a leg amputated. It was then, because he could no longer handle manual work, that he and his wife went into the provision business. Judge was known to be a heavy drinker and when under the influence could be very aggressive.

On 15 May 1886, Judge's wife announced that she was leaving him because of his heavy drinking. Jane stayed at her daughter's house for a few days and then returned home but Judge told her he did not want her back. Jane must have been a self sufficient woman because a short while later she opened an adjoining shop selling the same produce as her husband. This must have fuelled the fire that was already in Judge's nature.

On 7 July Judge bought a five-chambered revolver for 14s (70p) from Mr Mark's shop in Newcastle. He then went to a gunsmith and bought some ammunition. On 9 July he went to his wife's shop but she was not there so he left. Judge must have been watching for his wife because when Jane returned shortly afterwards he followed her into the shop. He called out to her, 'You'll die, you'll die'. When Jane heard this and saw the gun she tried to screen herself with a window shutter. A little girl, Judge's stepdaughter, was in the shop at the time. She saw Judge approach the spot where Jane was trying to hide herself and put his hand behind the shutter. There was the sound of a shot and as the little girl ran to get help she heard a second shot. By the time the neighbours arrived Jane was dead with two gunshot wounds to the head.

Judge gave himself up to PC Edward Tait saying that he had shot his wife twice because she had driven him to it. He added that he had tried to speak to his wife earlier but she would not have a kind word for him. Judge was arrested and on 10 July was examined by Dr Hardcastle, surgeon, at Newcastle Gaol. The doctor found that Judge had been drinking to excess and was suffering delirium due to the drink. Judge was sent to the infirmary and after a few days transferred to a cell. Dr Hardcastle was called upon again because Judge was claiming that there were people in the cell with him and they were going to hurt him. He was returned to the infirmary and received treatment but the episode repeated itself when he was once more put into a cell. The outcome was that he spent the time before his trial in the infirmary.

James Berry, assisted by John Morley, carried out the execution of Patrick Judge at Newcastle in 1875. Author's collection

Judge stood trial at the Newcastle Assizes before Justice Hawkins. It was already a certain fact that Judge had killed his wife but the jury must decide whether it was manslaughter or murder. Dr Hardcastle gave evidence that he had no doubt that drink was the cause of the disorder that Judge suffered. A man could do strange things while

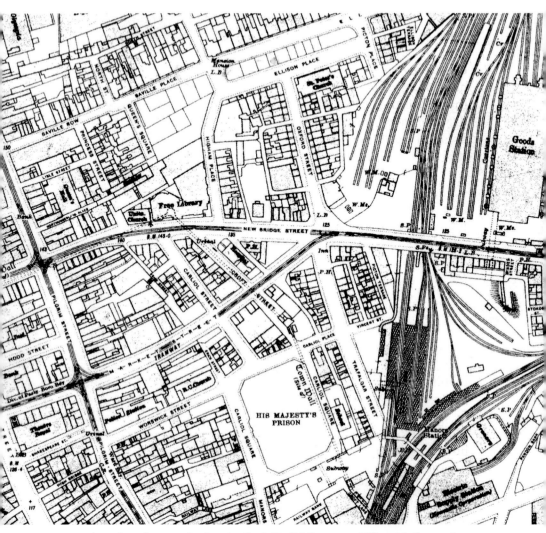

A portion of a map showing the Gaol, Carliol Square and Worswick Street where the crowds gathered to try and catch a glimpse of Patrick Judge's execution and to see the black flag hoisted at the moment of Judge's death in 1875. Ordnance Survey, Newcastle, 1914

suffering from delirium without realising what the consequences could be. It was pointed out by the prosecution that Judge had bought the gun but had not used it until two days later so it could have not been a rash act during a bout of drinking.

The defence used was the provocation that Judge endured prior to the shooting. The reasons given were that Jane had opened a shop and was hawking the same provisions as her husband. Jane was getting all the custom and depriving him of his livelihood. Judge's efforts at reconciliation were denied. All this had brought on a high state of mental excitement which drove him to a frenzy which caused him to commit the dreadful deed. It was also mentioned that having served in India, Judge had suffered from sunstroke and this could have been a factor contributing to his mental state.

The jury found Judge guilty of the murder of his wife and Justice Hawkins pronounced sentence of death. A petition for reprieve was drawn up stating the same arguments that the defence had used and it was signed by the people of his neighbourhood. A letter was written to the army to enquire about Judge's service record. The reply stated that there was no record of him ever having had sunstroke. The letter also stated that Judge's character whilst in the army was indifferent due to drunkenness and absence. The Home Secretary refused to intervene and grant a reprieve so Judge had to accept his fate. Judge could neither read nor write but he dictated a letter to his sister in which he thanked his neighbours for their support and the gaol officials for the kind manner in the way he had been treated. He had received comfort from Reverend Wood, a Roman Catholic priest, and wrote that because of this he would go to his death with a good heart.

James Berry, who was aged about thirty-four, and his assistant John George Morley were employed to carry out the execution. Executioners were considered celebrities by the lower and middle classes and knowing that their arrival in Newcastle would attract a crowd Berry and Morley decided to travel from Bradford the day prior to the execution and alight at Durham and board another train which would take them to Gateshead. They walked from there to Newcastle but their plan had been anticipated and there was a crowd waiting in Grainger Street to catch a glimpse of them. Berry always wore a tall hat and a dark suit covered by a greatcoat. He passed through his admirers without incident and entered the confines of the gaol.

Berry described Judge as, except for the wooden leg, a strong, good-looking man, who, in his soldier's uniform, must have cut an impressive figure.

Judge, at the age of forty-eight, was hanged within Newcastle Gaol on the morning of Tuesday, 16 November 1886. He met his doom with a crucifix held firmly in his hands and a prayer on his lips. This particular execution attracted an estimated 2,000 morbid spectators gathered along Worswick Street hoping to catch a glimpse of the proceedings and to see the black flag hoisted when the sentence was complete. Later Berry was said to be quite upset because he had hanged 'a poor cripple'.

CHAPTER 21

Immoral Behaviour?
1890

He [Berry] placed the rope around the beam and attached a bag of sand to it, to be jerked down the cavity of the scaffold.

Lily McClarence Wilson, otherwise Myers, had lived in Manchester with her husband, John Myers, a water cart carrier, and their son. In 1889 Lily met William Row, a shoemaker, who was also married and had a son. Row's son, Harry, and Lily's son, John, were both about eight when the couple decided they wished to start a new life together so, taking the two boys, they left their respective partners in Manchester and moved to Newcastle. It was October, 1889.

Helen Tait kept a lodging house at 4 Pine Street in Newcastle where Row and his paramour went looking for accommodation. They told Mrs Tait that their previous partners were both dead and they had been married to each other for about a year. Mrs Tait rented the family a room in her house and they seemed to be quite happy until Christmas Eve of that year when the couple were heard quarrelling bitterly. By the following day the dispute had blown over and things went back to normal.

It was late afternoon on 3 January when the peace of the lodging house was really shattered. Lily's son, John, had gone on an errand and Harry was playing in an adjoining room. Row had come in from work and Lily had put a steak in the frying pan for his tea. She had then gone into Mrs Tait's kitchen to boil a kettle. Shortly after Lily had returned to her own room Mrs Tait heard a scream and the sound of breaking dishes. She stopped what she was doing and listened for a moment. When Mrs Tait heard a second scream she went to investigate. Young John Myers had returned from his errand and reached the scene before the landlady. He was standing in the middle of the room crying and shouting 'Mama'. Mrs Tait saw Lily lying on the floor with Row bending over her. Assuming Row was hitting his wife Mrs Tait grabbed his arm to pull him away. She then heard the boy shout that Row was cutting his mother's throat. Mrs Tait then realised that Row had a knife in his hand and that Lily was covered in blood. She shouted at John to get help and he ran out of the house and into the street. Meanwhile Row donned his hat and coat and calmly left the house.

PC Rose happened to be walking his beat at the time and, hearing children crying, was already heading in the direction of the front door of the lodging house. John shouted to the policeman that his mother had been murdered. PC Rose followed John into the house to find that Lily was indeed dead. Beside the body was a razor-sharp shoemaker's knife. Dr Cross was called and on examination of the body found six knife wounds, two of which were deep enough to have caused almost instant death. Row had gone straight to the Westgate police station and told the constable on duty that he had just committed a murder.

Row stood trial on 21 February 1890 before Justice Grantham. Mrs Tait told the court what she had seen on 3 January and added that on the previous Christmas Eve Row had been drinking but did not seem very drunk. The couple had argued loudly that night. The chief witness was young John Myers. He told the court that on Christmas Eve his mother had been laughing and singing with two young men and Row had become very angry and ordered them to leave. His mother and Row had continued to argue long after the visitors were gone and the situation had remained very tense until the final fatal outcome.

Row's defence was that Lily had been unfaithful to him and that she had obtained money by prostituting herself. The anger had been building up within him since Christmas Eve. It was not ascertained whether there had been any additional

A portion of a map showing the location of Pine Street where William Row murdered his paramour in 1890. Ordnance Survey, Newcastle and Gateshead, 1894

provocation from Lily to drive Row into stabbing her that day. It was suggested that he had brought the knife home with him from work with the premeditated intention of killing Lily.

The jury were out for two hours and thirty-five minutes before returning a verdict of guilty of wilful murder but with a recommendation for mercy. Justice Grantham pointed out that Row had encouraged Lily to be unfaithful to her previous man so had no excuse for anger if she had done the same to him. There was certainly no justification for taking her life in such a brutal manner so there was no other option than to pronounce sentence of death.

Several petitions for mercy were forwarded to the Home Secretary but intervention was declined as there were not sufficient grounds to interfere with the due course of the law. Row had shown a somewhat indifferent manner after the trial. It was thought that this was because he held out a strong hope that a reprieve would be forthcoming. When he was told there was to be no reprieve his bravado crumbled and he became very upset.

The executioner, James Berry, arrived at Newcastle Central Station on the afternoon of the day prior to the execution and was met by an official. Soon after he arrived at the gaol Berry inspected the scaffold. He placed the rope around the beam and attached a bag of sand to it, to be jerked down the cavity of the scaffold. This was to test that the rope would stand the strain of holding Row's weight.

On the morning of Wednesday, 12 March at Newcastle Gaol forty-year-old William Row was hanged for the murder of Lily McClarence Wilson.

CHAPTER 22

The Power of the Pen
1894

...Emery had gone to the gallows calm and totally unafraid.

O n the churchyard wall of Holy Saviour's Church in Tynemouth are carved the initials MM and a heart, a symbol of young love, but in this case a memoriam to tragedy. The initials belonged to Mary Ann Marshall who did not live long enough to see love blossom past its first spring.

Mary, better known as Polly, lived at Cross Street in Tynemouth with her father, Robert, who worked for the

Tynemouth Priory where Samuel Emery and Polly Marshall would stroll whilst declaring their love for one another in 1894. Author's collection

Tynemouth Corporation. Samuel George Emery came from West Bromwich and was a private in the South Staffordshire Regiment. In 1894 his regiment was stationed at Tynemouth Barracks. Emery was twenty and Polly seventeen when they met and became smitten with each other. They wanted to marry but, because of Polly's age, without parental consent could not do so. Between Whitley Bay and Tynemouth there was a walking route called the Broadway which led to Holy Saviour's Church and was a favourite haunt for young couples. At some point in their courtship they carved a heart and her initials into the wall surrounding the churchyard. The engraving, although faded, has survived to the present day. For a time the couple spent every minute they could together, often walking along the Broadway until they reached the shadow of the church, but their happiness was suddenly cut short when Emery was transferred to Strensall near York. The distance was too far for them to see each other so the only communication available was by letter so, for a time, this would have to be sufficient.

How surprised Polly must have been when, in July, she received a letter from the love of her life telling her she had better watch what she was doing or he would turn up when she least expected. It appeared that, besides letters from Polly, Emery had received another from an unknown source. The writer suggested that Polly 'was seeing another man'. Nearly 100 miles from his sweetheart, Emery's imagination as to what she was up to must have run riot. His jealousy was then fuelled further by another letter. Emery deserted on Saturday, 21 July and headed for Tynemouth. He saw Polly on Saturday and was in her house on Sunday having abandoned his soldier's uniform for civilian dress. On Monday, 23 July Emery went to the post office and sent a form of letter-telegram to Polly asking her to meet him that evening. It later transpired that he had also paid a visit to Thomas Moar's ironmonger's shop where he had purchased a large clasp knife and asked for it to be sharpened.

That evening Emery and Polly met in Percy Park and walked towards Holy Saviour's Church. Reverend Nichols was on his tricycle, also heading towards the church, when he saw what appeared to be 'two boys playing'. He then realised it was not play but a desperate struggle. Nichols saw a man strike a person lying on the ground two or three times then run off towards the back of the railway station. Polly was on her feet by now but was bleeding profusely from a deep cut in her neck. Her hands were also badly lacerated where, presumably, she had tried to defend herself against the attack. Nichols took Polly into the vestry but she died minutes later. Other people were passing by and had witnessed the attack. Two men chased after the assailant. One, James Gibson, caught up with Emery who turned and threatened him with a knife. Gibson was later to say that Emery had the 'appearance of a madly desperate man'. The chase continued but Gibson lost Emery at the railway sidings.

Later that evening Emery entered the *Crescent Tavern* in Hudson Street. By this time the attack was on everyone's lips. He asked someone if the victim had died and he was told that she had. Emery then asked the landlady for a pencil and paper. After writing something down he placed it in an envelope and asked the landlady to give him a few minutes before she read the note. Emery had written a confession. Later that night two police officers apprehended Emery, still holding the knife, near the House of Correction in Tynemouth.

Emery stood trial at Newcastle Assizes on 20 November before Justice Charles. He took full responsibility for his actions so it was an easy task for the jury. The verdict of guilty was returned with no recommendation for mercy and sentence of death was pronounced.

Emery wrote to Polly's father asking for forgiveness for his act. Perhaps at the end he realised that there had been no real cause for the mistrust of his sweetheart. Who wrote the letters, or indeed if there ever were any such letters, never came to light but if the letters were not a figment of Emery's jealous imagination then the person who wrote them must have surely gone to the grave with a terrible weight on their conscience.

Samuel Emery was hanged within Newcastle Gaol on 11 December 1894 and his body interred within the confines of the gaol. The executioner, James Billington, said afterwards that Emery had gone to the gallows calm and totally unafraid.

CHAPTER 23

Murder at Cullercoats
1901

*The next thing she knew her husband was lying
dead on the floor ...*

The Miller family had been hawkers all their working lives travelling from one end of the country to the other. In a combination of good selling techniques, hard work and careful saving they managed to buy property in Cullercoats. The elder John Miller and his second wife, Mary, bought a house at 55 Hudlestone Street. Mr Miller died in about 1893 leaving Mary a fairly well-to-do widow. The house was divided into two with Mary occupying the top floor flat. Joseph Ferguson and his son were lodgers in Mary's house. The son moved away and, after a time, Joseph Ferguson and Mary became a couple and married in about 1897. Mary changed her will leaving everything to her new husband so perhaps this upset some of her family. Mary, by virtue of having been the second wife of John Miller, was stepmother to her deceased husband's son, John, who was about seven years older than her new husband. John Miller was quite a well-known figure as he owned fairground rides at Tynemouth. He often kept company with his nephew, John Robert Miller, who was a travelling musician. In 1901 John Miller was sixty-seven and his nephew thirty-one so Ferguson would have been about sixty.

On the afternoon of Friday, 20 September uncle and nephew called at a shop in Saville Street, North Shields. The elder Miller asked the owner of the shop, George Purvis, if they could look at some knives. He told Purvis that his nephew was going to sea as a ship's cook and would need a specific type of knife. A knife and sheath were chosen and paid for with the younger Miller putting it in his pocket as he left the shop.

The Long Sands at Tynemouth where John Miller had his fairground rides.
Author's collection

Later that afternoon the two Millers were seen by a cab driver entering the *Bay Hotel* and leaving a few minutes later and heading towards Hudlestone Street. The cab driver later stated that the pair looked as though they were drunk especially the younger Miller who appeared to stagger along the street. The story was then taken up by a thirteen-year-old boy, Robert Stephenson Oliver, who saw the two men approach the front door of the Ferguson's house in Huddlestone Street. Oliver saw the younger Miller knock on the door while his uncle tucked himself into the doorway of the next house out of sight of anyone answering the door of the Ferguson's house. When the door was opened by John Ferguson the two men rushed inside and the door was quickly closed. This rather odd behaviour was also witnessed by James Melvin who had a grocery shop opposite to the Ferguson house. After a few minutes Melvin heard Mary Ferguson at an upstairs window calling to a boy who was passing by to knock on a neighbour's door and ask her to come out. When the neighbour appeared Mary asked her to fetch the police.

PC Whitehead was on duty at the time and arrived at the house very soon afterwards to find the front door locked. He knocked but it was not until he shouted who he was that Mary would open the door. When Constable Whitehead entered the house he saw the body of Joseph Ferguson lying at the foot of the stairs. A bloodstained knife was also found on the property. Meanwhile the two perpetrators had left by the rear

The Bay Hotel *where the Millers had been drinking prior to the murder of John Ferguson.* Author's collection

entrance of the house but by this time a small crowd of people had already gathered there to see what was going on. The grocer, Melvin, having watched the two Millers acting so oddly, told the crowd not to let them leave. When Constable Whitehead came out of the house the arrest of the two men was made easy for him as they had been detained by the neighbours. The pair were taken to North Shields police station and charged with murder.

An initial inquest was held at the *Bay Hotel* and five police court appearances followed before the two men were committed for trial at the Assizes. The trial was held at the Moot Hall before Justice Grantham on 15 November 1901.

In what was described as 'a frenzied attack' Joseph Ferguson had sustained six knife wounds to his face and neck and two on his hand, probably inflicted as he tried to ward off the attack. The evidence from witnesses putting the two men at the scene was overwhelming. The question was whether only one or both were guilty and what was the motive. Mary Ferguson testified that the events had happened so quickly she was not absolutely sure of what had taken place after her husband had opened the door. Mary had been standing at the top of the stairs and thought that the elder Miller had bolted the front door after they had burst in while the younger Miller seemed to be fighting with her husband. The next thing she knew her husband was lying dead on the floor and the two men came up the stairs into her flat and then ran down a second set of stairs that led to the back entrance of the building. Mary could think of no motive for the attack. She said that as far as she knew there had been no bad feeling amongst the parties involved. Mary could not even believe it was jealousy over her money as she had always been generous to her stepson and his nephew.

The elder Miller insisted that he had nothing to do with the attack and had, in fact, tried to prevent it. His nephew admitted to stabbing the victim but insisted it was because his uncle had given him drink and goaded him into committing the act. John Robert also said that he was not responsible for his actions as he had been kicked in the head by a horse when he was young and now suffered from severe headaches.

Huddlestone Street where the murder of John Ferguson took place. Author's collection

After due deliberation, a verdict of guilty was returned by the jury on both men. Justice Grantham donned the black cap and pronounced the death sentence. The younger Miller's solicitor appealed to the Home Secretary for a reprieve on the grounds of his client's mental state. The appeal was denied and a date was set for the sentence to be carried out.

Usually where more than one felon was to be executed the hangings would be carried out together but as the day became closer the young Miller became more and more distressed and, in fact, hysterical. The authorities decided it would be easier for all concerned if the two men were hanged separately. On Saturday, 7 December the elder Miller was escorted from the condemned cell to the scaffold within Newcastle Gaol and hanged at 8 am. His last words were that he was innocent. The younger Miller then followed in the last footsteps of his uncle. In his final minutes John Robert appeared to have divorced himself from reality as he asked what all the people were doing

JOHN MILLER   JOHN ROBERT MILLER.

A sketch of John and John Robert Miller at their trial in 1901. Author's collection

there. He dropped through the trap at 9.30am. The hangings had been carried out by William Billington assisted by his younger brother, John, and John Ellis. This was John Ellis's first execution.

CHAPTER 24

An Unprovoked Attack
1905

John Ellis adjusted the ankle strap while Henry Pierrepoint placed the white cap over his head.

In the early evening of Thursday, 13 July, at a lodging house situated at 94 Newgate Street in Newcastle, a drunken feud culminated in murder. One of the residents of the house was Henry Perkins. He was forty and a cobbler by trade, working for John Proctor in Church Street, Walker. Another lodger was a twenty-nine-year-old Irishman, Patrick Durkin. He worked as a mason's labourer and had only been living in the lodging house for a few weeks. It soon became common knowledge in the house that Perkins and Durkin were rather fond of a dram or two.

On Wednesday, 12 July, Annie Jackson, charwoman at the lodging house, had seen the pair fighting in the lavatory and then outside in the lane. Later they began to scuffle on the staircase and Perkins had pulled a knife from somewhere on his person. William Harris, the manager of the lodging house, managed to grab Perkins by the arm in time to stop him stabbing Durkin. Harris took no further action because the two men were so drunk, a decision which he would later regret. The following evening Durkin returned to the house and fell asleep in a drunken stupor on the wooden bench in the kitchen. About half an hour later, at around 7.30 pm, Perkins came in to the kitchen also very drunk and making a terrific racket. Annie, who was pottering about in the kitchen finishing off her chores, asked him to be quiet as Durkin was asleep and she did not want a repeat of the previous arguments between the two men. Annie then saw something in Perkins' hand and asked what it was. He told her it was a newspaper. Perkins then walked over to the sleeping Durkin and, putting a knee on his chest, lifted his arm holding what Annie could now see was a shoemaker's knife. Annie, in a brave but rather foolhardy gesture, pulled Perkins away and then ran for Harris. The two of them got back to the kitchen too late to prevent the tragedy. Durkin was feebly trying to stand up while blood gushed from a wound to his throat. His attacker was nowhere to be seen having left by the exit door.

Perkins, still very drunk, went to the shop where he worked and told his employer that he had stabbed a man. Proctor tried to get Perkins to sit down but he left the shop. Proctor called the police and Perkins was arrested by PC Walter Wood in the city centre early the following morning and charged with unlawful wounding.

Meanwhile Durkin had been taken to the Newcastle Infirmary with two wounds to his throat, one of which had severed an artery. He died from his injuries on 19 July. This

Victoria Infirmary in 1909. It was here that Durkin was taken in 1905 for treatment after he was stabbed by Henry Perkins. He died of his injuries a few days later. Author's collection

changed the charge against Perkins to murder. After three police court appearances Perkins was committed to stand trial on 16 November at Newcastle Assizes before Justice Darling.

Besides the charwoman and the manager from the lodging house the two men who had shared the room with Perkins and Durkin gave testimony. They stated there had been bad feeling between the two since Durkin had moved in. Another witness, James Healey, told the court that he had spoken to Perkins on the day of the murder and that he had said he was 'going to do for Durkin'. Apparently this feud had started when Perkins had said that he had £4,000 savings and Durkin had called him a liar. It had been a lie because Perkins did not even have the means to pay for his own defence. Perkins' version of events was totally different. He stated that Durkin had attacked him and he had retaliated. Because the knife was in his hand Durkin had been cut and it was an accident. The jury did not believe his story and found him guilty of murder. An appeal for reprieve was sent to the Home Secretary but was denied. Perkins never made a formal confession but did write to a friend saying that he deserved to die for what he had done.

The execution took place within Newcastle Gaol on Wednesday, 6 December 1905. At just before 8 am Perkins was led to the scaffold. John Ellis adjusted the ankle strap while Henry Pierrepoint placed the white cap over his head. Pierrepoint then quickly drew the bolt and Perkins shot out of sight. The rope gave a slight twitch and then was taut. Perkins had gone to his death without a murmur.

The media had printed that Perkins had no visitors whilst being held before his execution. This was denied by a Mr Fred Franks of Brinkburn Street in Newcastle. After the execution he wrote to the *Newcastle Daily Chronicle* saying that he wished to contradict that statement. He had been a friend of the family for many years and, along with four other men, had visited Perkins on more than one occasion whilst he was awaiting his fate.

CHAPTER 25

The End of the Line
1910

... under the seat was the body of a man.

On Friday, 18 March a train, consisting of three carriages and a luggage van, left Newcastle Railway Station at 10.27am. After travelling about thirty-four miles and making fourteen stops the train pulled into Alnmouth at just after noon. When Thomas Charlton, the porter, boarded the train for his usual inspection to make sure the carriages were left clean he saw what looked like blood on the floor of a third class compartment. On further investigation, to his horror, under the seat was the body of a man. Near to the body were a hat and a pair of broken spectacles. It was quite obvious the man had not died from natural causes and the police were immediately alerted.

Newcastle Railway Station in the nineteenth century. Author's collection

The body was removed and examined by a doctor who found that there were five bullet wounds to the head. The bullets were of two different sizes so it was thought two guns had been used. According to the doctor any one of the bullets would have caused death. The victim was identified as John Innes Nisbet, a forty-four-year-old colliery pay clerk who lived with his wife and two daughters at 180 Heaton Road, Heaton.

Nisbet had worked for Messrs Rayne & Burn, Beaconsfield Chambers, Sandhill for over twenty years. One of his duties every alternate Friday was to cash a cheque from his employers and then take the money to Stobswood Colliery, near Widdrington, to be paid out in wages. On the day he was killed he had followed his usual routine and called into Lloyds Bank on Collingwood Street where he cashed a cheque for £370 9s 6d (£370.48p). The cash, which was in gold, sovereigns and copper, was then put into a leather bag and Nisbet proceeded to the station to catch his train. When the body was found there was no sign of the bag or money. The police immediately launched an investigation and witness statements pointed to seeing a man talking to Nisbet on the station but the description given could have fitted almost anyone, 5ft 6ins tall, not very old and sallow complexion. Nisbet's wife, Cicely, usually waited at Heaton Station and had a word with her husband before the train left and if he had been paid his wages he would give the money to her. The only thing different on 18 March was that he was sitting further up the train than usual and she had to look for him. Mrs Nisbet spoke to her husband through the train window. She had seen another man in the compartment but, according to her first statement, not clearly enough to know who he was as the collar of his overcoat was turned up and he was sitting on the far side of the compartment in the shadows. Later, at the inquest, Mrs Nisbet fainted and afterwards said it was because she recognised the prisoner as the man that had been in the compartment with her husband. It transpired, though not at the trial, that Mrs Nisbet had not disclosed that she had known Dickman for years and had seen him just days before the murder. Surely if he had been the man Mrs Nisbet had seen in the train she would have recognised him. If this had

Newcastle Railway Station in 1905. It was from here that the train left for Alnmouth in 1910, with John Nisbet as a passenger. Author's collection

come out at the trial it would have raised serious doubts on the identity of the man travelling with Nisbet.

A reward of £100 was offered by Stobswood Colliery for information leading to the arrest of the murderer. When the newspapers released the story with a description of Nisbet and a public appeal for witnesses William Hepple, from Acclington, contacted the police and told them he had seen a man he knew, Alexander John Dickman, with a slightly built man fitting the description of the victim. He said they were talking together on the station and then walked to the train as if they were both about to board although he did not see them actually get onto the train together.

This was enough for the police to give them a suspect. On 21 March the police paid a visit to Dickman at his home at 1 Lily Avenue, Jesmond and asked him to accompany them back to the police station. Dickman told the police he was on the train but had not travelled in the same compartment as Nisbet and that beside a cursory good morning on the station there had been no more conversation between them. He said he had meant to alight from the train at Stannington but was reading the racing page and missed his stop so alighted at Morpeth instead. Dickman said he then began to walk to Stannington but felt ill so returned to Morpeth and caught the 1.40pm train back to Newcastle. Dickman's story was backed up by William Sanderson who had seen Dickman in Morpeth and stated that he was acting normally and certainly not like a man who had just murdered someone in cold blood. Dickman was the only suspect the police had and he was arrested for the murder. During the time before the trial the police continued to gather evidence against Dickman including holding a line-up of nine men for identification by witnesses. Percival Hall, a colliery clerk, had seen Nisbet and another man board the train. He and John Spink, another witness, were asked to attend the line-up to see if they could identify Nisbet's companion. The two witnesses were given a sneak preview of Dickman through a partially open door before seeing the nine men lined up together. This was not forthcoming at the trial. After viewing the line-up Hall told the police that one of the men 'could have been' or 'resembled' the man he had seen. He then said if he was assured that the murderer was amongst the nine men then he could pick out the prisoner, which he did. Spink stated he could not positively identify anyone. If the facts of this line-up 'identification' had come out at the trial this would have also cast serious doubts on the validity of identity.

On 18 June the leather bag that Nisbet had been carrying was found in an air shaft of the Isabella Pit at Hepscott Colliery, which was just over a mile from Stannington. The bag had been cut open and the money, except for a few coppers, was gone. The prosecution suggested that Dickman was familiar with this pit and the fact that it was disused because of water problems. Dickman denied knowing anything about that particular pit and said he had been nowhere near the vicinity.

The bullets that had been used to shoot Nisbet were found to be of two different types and sizes so it was thought two

Alnmouth as it would have been in 1910 when John Nisbet was found murdered on the Newcastle to Alnmouth train. Author's collection

different weapons had been used. It can now be certain that the bullets were fired from the same weapon. The smaller ones had been packed, probably with paper, to make them fit. There were two connections to Dickman concerning a gun. Dickman used the name Fred Black and an address at a newsagent in the Groat Market for his betting slips. The assistant, Henrietta Hyman, stated that a strange parcel that looked as though it may have contained a gun was received for 'Fred Black' from Bell Brothers in Glasgow. A few weeks later a postcard arrived with another parcel from the same firm saying the first parcel had been sent in error and should be returned. The assistant gave Dickman a label to return the parcel but did not know if he had done so. The other connection was an entry in a register from W R Pape & Co Gunsmiths of Newcastle. The entry showed that Dickman had bought a gun there in 1907.

When the police searched Dickman's home they found gloves and a pair of trousers both with spots of blood on them. Except to say that the blood was fairly fresh it could not be proved whose it was or even if it was human. There were also stains on one of Dickman's overcoats that looked as though something had been rubbed off with paraffin. The prosecution suggested that this had also been bloodstained. Dickman had just over £17 in his possession, a large proportion of it in gold. On checking his financial situation the police found, although he had been quite affluent in the past, he was now struggling and had pawned jewellery and borrowed money recently. Dickman told the police that the money he had came from betting.

Dickman's trial began on 4 July and was to last three days. The trial took place at the Moot Hall at Newcastle before Justice Coleridge. Hundreds of people crowded about the courthouse trying to gain admission. Their efforts were in vain, the seats were filled with witnesses and others directly

Lily Avenue in Jesmond as it would have looked when Alexander Dickman lived there in the early twentieth century. Author's collection

involved in the case, including Mrs Nisbet and Mrs Dickman, with the remaining seats allocated to members of the press and a few privileged people. Prosecuting for the Crown were Tindal Atkinson, KC and C F Lowenthal. Edward Mitchell Innes, KC and Lord William Percy represented Dickman.

Perhaps if Dickman had not gone onto the stand to try and speak in his own defence the outcome of the trial may have been different. He did not make a good impression on the jury. He admitted knowing of the routine for the payment of the colliery wages, but so did many others. Dickman explained that he suffered from piles and it was that condition that had caused him to feel ill and alight from the train at Morpeth. When all the evidence had been heard the judge's summing up contained an inference towards Dickman being responsible for the crime. The jury deliberated for two and a half hours before returning a verdict of guilty. Before pronouncing sentence of death Justice Coleridge spoke to Dickman:

> *Prisoner at the bar a patient and careful trial is now at an end. The irrevocable decision has now been given. The jury have found you guilty of the crime of murder. In your hunger and lust for gold you had no pity upon the victim who you slew. It is only just that the Nemesis of the law should overtake the author of the crime.*

When the judge had finished speaking Dickman stated to the court 'I declare to all men I am innocent'. The whole case was based on circumstantial evidence. Dickman was not positively identified as the man being in the same compartment as the victim. Hepple was the only person that supposedly saw Dickman and Nisbet walking towards the train together. No weapon was ever found, no blood match ever made and, except for the £17 Dickman had at the time of his arrest, no money was recovered. Mrs Dickman had used paraffin to remove some oil stains from her husband's coat but she was not called upon for this evidence. Much of the trial centered on Dickman saying that when he left the train at Morpeth he began to walk to Stannington but took ill. It was alleged that he had used this time to dump the money bag in the pit shaft. A great deal of emphasis was also made of his financial situation. Dickman admitted to knowing about the wages Nisbet was carrying and never denied talking to him or being on the same train but protested his innocence to the murder. Many were surprised at the outcome of the trial and an appeal was launched. By this time it had become public knowledge that the police had tampered with the evidence, so to speak, in the way the line-up was carried out. It made the positive identification of Dickman questionable. Even though this and other doubts on some of the evidence came to light at the appeal it was turned down. A petition for reprieve was sent to the Home Secretary, who at that time was Winston Churchill, but this too was denied.

Whether Dickman was guilty or not there was certainly a 'reasonable doubt'. His trial was a farce and he should never have been convicted on the severely flawed evidence that was presented.

Early on the morning of Tuesday, 9 August 1910 a huge crowd of over a thousand people had gathered outside the prison hoping to catch a glimpse of the forthcoming event which was to take place at 8 am. They were, however, disappointed as a screen had been erected hiding the route from the cell to the place of execution. In the final minutes the prison chaplain, Reverend W F Lumley, implored Dickman to tell the truth and go to his death with a clear conscience. Alexander John Dickman, at the age of forty-four, still swearing to his innocence, walked to the gallows within Newcastle Gaol to be hanged by John Ellis and his assistant, William Willis.

CHAPTER 26

A Triple Murder at Bedlington 1913

While waiting for his sentence to be carried out Amos turned to religion ...

ohn Vickers Amos was thirty-five and married to Isabella. The couple had three children, the youngest three and the oldest eleven. Jocker, as he was commonly known, had worked as a miner since he was a boy and had never been in trouble. He was working in a mine in Alabama when there was an explosion which killed two men and injured others. He had been burned while rescuing two men. Later that same year Amos was in another explosion where lives were lost. This affected him deeply and perhaps even disturbed his mind. These events probably prompted Amos to look for a safer line of work. He returned to England

The Sun Inn *at Bedlington as it looked in 1913 when the murder of a woman and two policemen took place.* Newcastle Illustrated Chronicle

and, after paying a £30 bond, became landlord of the *Sun Inn* on Front Street in Bedlington in January 1913. James Irons from Newcastle owned the inn and did a stock check once a month. On the first stock check Irons told Amos that there was a shortfall of over £7. Irons did two more checks and by 6 April told Amos that the shortfall now amounted to nearly £46. Amos protested that it could not be possible as all the money was put into the till. Irons told Amos that he only had until 15 April to sort things out or something would have to be done. True to his word, on Tuesday, 15 April, Irons brought in a professional stocktaker and Amos knew his days as a landlord were over. When he asked Irons about the return of his bond he was told it would depend on the stocktaker's findings. Amos could see his hard earned money slipping away and on top of that he and his family were to be thrown out of their accommodation. In a twist of fate perhaps, as the stock check was ongoing, Mrs Amos appeared with her husband's Winchester shotgun saying a customer wanted to borrow it. Amos told her that the gun was not to be lent to anyone. It

Sarah Grice, one of the murder victims, outside her house at the lodge at Seghill Hall before she went to Bedlington with her husband to take over the management of the Sun Inn. Newcastle Illustrated Chronicle

Sarah Grice's son. Newcastle Illustrated Chronicle

seems that Amos then sent his son, George, out to buy cartridges for the gun. By now Irons was becoming worried that his evacuation of the Amos family from the premises was going to be difficult so he went to the police station and was told a constable would be sent along to make sure that everything went peacefully. Irons then went to the railway station to collect Richard Grice who was to take over as landlord from Amos. When the two men arrived back at the inn Irons must have known the situation was becoming worse. He returned to the police station to hurry some official help along. Constable John Mussell accompanied Irons, first to collect Mrs Sarah Ellen Grice and her belongings, then to the inn. The events that followed are a little hazy but it is thought that the stock check now complete, Irons told Amos there was an even larger shortfall than previously and he was to leave the premises immediately. Even though Amos had seen this coming it still must have taken a few minutes to sink in. Amos had then gone upstairs and reappeared carrying the shotgun. As he returned with the gun he was confronted by Constable Mussell who tried to reason with him but Amos was past all reason. He fired the gun twice and the constable received a bullet to his chest and neck. Irons disappeared through the cellar hatch while Mrs Grice began screaming. Amos fired at the innocent woman and her screams were cut short as a gaping wound, exposing her brain, appeared in the back of her head. People began running towards the inn when they heard the commotion. Amongst them was Sergeant Andrew Barton who ran straight into the inn through the back door with a number of other men close behind. Amos fired the gun again and Sergeant Barton fell to the ground having taken the shot in the chest. The men that were behind him ran back out and around to the front of the inn.

At the police station re-inforcements were rounded up and headed for the crime scene. Amos stood at the front door for a while still brandishing the gun and making threats saying he had two cartridges left, one for Irons and one for himself. No one dared approach and it gave Amos time to leave by the back

Isabella Amos, whose husband was convicted of the murder of three people at the Sun Inn *at Bedlington in 1913.*
Newcastle Illustrated Chronicle

door and disappear into the fields.

A search by locals and police was launched and later that evening one of the searchers spotted a footprint in the grass beside a culvert in Church Bank. The police instructed Joe Potter, a miner, to fire into the culvert. Amos shouted that he would surrender but then there was total silence. Potter fired a second shot and there was a shout and Amos came out of the culvert. The second shot had grazed his forehead. When his shotgun was retrieved it was found to be jammed which probably saved some of the searchers' lives and perhaps stopped him taking his own life.

The trial was held at Newcastle on 2 and 3 July before Commissioner Harrison. Although there had been three murders, because it was a capital crime, Amos was only charged with one, that of Constable Barton. Irons's testimony was that he had never accused the Amos family of stealing but only held them responsible for the shortfall. It was shown that Irons sold his barrels of beer at such a high price with no allowance for wastage that Amos would lose approximately £1

Joe Potter, the miner, who fired the two shots into the culvert and caused Amos to come out and give himself up. Newcastle Illustrated Chronicle

Sergeant Alexander Barton, one of the three murder victims. Author's collection

per day. The more beer Amos sold the more money he would lose and the more Irons would gain. Perhaps Amos was no good with book-keeping and was not able to see where he was going wrong. He only knew that he had been perfectly honest with the takings. He pleaded that the policemen were his friends and he was insane at the time of the murders, and he probably was. Irons said that he paid Amos two weeks wages and commission amounting to a little more than £3. Amos denied that he had received any money at all from Irons. The only money that was found on Amos when he was arrested was a sovereign. Whatever the provocation the fact remained that Amos had shot a woman and two policemen in cold blood and the jury could do no other but find him guilty. A huge

NORTH EASTERN POLICE HISTORY SOCIETY
in association with
NORTHUMBRIA POLICE,
WANSBECK DISTRICT COUNCIL and
BEDLINGTON CHAMBER OF COMMERCE
wish to announce

A CEREMONY OF

𝕽emembrance

TO REDEDICATE THE MEMORIAL STONE IN BEDLINGTON CEMETERY, ERECTED BY NORTHUMBERLAND COUNTY CONSTABULARY TO THE MEMORY OF

SERGEANT ANDREW BARTON
and
CONSTABLE GEORGE BERTRAM MUSSELL

Killed in the execution of their duty in the SUN INN,
BEDLINGTON on Tuesday the 15th April 1913.

ALL are welcome to attend the rededication ceremony of the newly refurbished memorial stone at 2.30pm on
SUNDAY, 13th APRIL 2003

The poster that was printed for the rededication of the memorial stone to the two policemen who were killed by Amos in 1913. Author's collection

petition was signed and the Northumberland miners sent a plea to the Home Secretary and the King for the sentence of death to be commuted to a prison sentence but to no avail.

While waiting for his sentence to be carried out Amos turned to religion and was baptised in gaol. His last letter was to his wife asking her to thank everyone for their support and kindness. John Vickers Amos was hanged at Newcastle on Tuesday, 22 July by Thomas Pierrepoint assisted by William Willis.

Sarah Grice was thirty-three and probably looking forward to a new life in a new place. George Bertram Mussell was thirty-one, married and had joined the police force in 1905. Andrew Barton was forty, married with two sons and had joined the police force in 1894. He had held a medal for gallantry for saving the life of a sailor during a shipwreck in 1907. The police officers' wives received the King's Police Medal in honour of the bravery of their husbands. Neither widow was awarded a pension.

The three victims were buried on 18 April in Bedlington cemetery. A memorial stone to the two police officers was erected in the cemetery in 1913 by the Northumberland Constabulary. In 2002 a retired police officer from Leeds was visiting Northumberland and looking around Bedlington cemetery came across the memorial stone which had, over the years, become sadly neglected. He contacted a member of the North East Police History Society who in turn contacted a stonemason. It was decided that the stone could be restored at a reasonable cost. The people of Bedlington, the District Council, Chamber of Trades and local historians all became involved in the project. In 2003 the restoration of the memorial stone was complete and a rededication ceremony was held on the 90th anniversary of the police officers' deaths.

CHAPTER 27

The Night Began Well
1917

... he walked to his doom with firm steps.

I n 1917 the First World War was still being fought and to most people's way of thinking there was too much death in Britain without murder taking place over trivialities. On Wednesday, 20 June four petty officers from the Royal Navy had been given shore leave whilst their ship was berthed at Newcastle. Alfred Gough, Grant, McDonald and Alfred Birling were having a drink in the *Mechanic's Arms* in Temple Street at about 8 pm. As the night went on the group became larger as two women joined the four sailors. They were Isabella Smith, whose husband was serving in France, and Sarah Shearer. A little later Ruby Wright and Margaret Brown came into the company and then another sailor, Henry Arthur Hollyer, who was twenty-seven, also sat down within the group. At closing time Ruby suggested they all go to her house at 1 West Street, which was close by, for a drink. Not wanting the night to end all concerned readily agreed. Ruby and her eight guests were thoroughly enjoying themselves when two more men turned up at about 11.30pm. They were James Innes and William James Thompson whose real name was William Cavanagh. Twenty-nine-year-old Cavanagh was introduced as Ruby's husband. A bottle of whisky was produced and the party carried on.

At sometime around midnight one of the ladies made a cutting remark aimed at Cavanagh and Innes referring to them not fighting for their country as these five brave naval men were. The remark sparked an argument between the two civilians and the sailors. As was to be expected tempers flared and fists began to fly. Cavanagh punched Hollyer, knocking him to the floor. When Innes and McDonald began to fight Gough went to intervene. Cavanagh pulled out a knife and stabbed Gough in the face. Ruby joined in the affray by throwing glasses at the seamen. Some of the company went outside but at some point Cavanagh had already stabbed Hollyer.

The police were called and when two officers arrived it was to find Hollyer lying in the back yard bleeding from a number of wounds. Hollyer, along with Innes, McDonald and Gough were taken to hospital. The police charged Cavanagh with wounding and Ruby Wright with assault. At a court hearing they were remanded in custody for eight days.

On Monday, 25 June Hollyer died from his injuries. He had been stabbed five times, in the neck, back, side and over the heart twice. Wright, Innes and Cavanagh were all charged with murder.

The trial was held at Newcastle Assizes on 12 November before Justice Salter. Edward Short, for the prosecution, decided there was not enough evidence against Ruby Wright so she was found not guilty leaving the two men to face the murder charge. The four surviving seamen testified that they were not

Newcastle Quayside, where the ships would berth and the sailors come ashore on leave. Author's collection

drunk and the only drink consumed at the house was a bottle of whisky which Wright had produced. Alfred Gough stated that after Cavanagh had stabbed him in the face with a penknife he had seen him bend down and stab the still recumbent Hollyer in the back. Wright testified that the seamen were drunk and had taken four bottles of whisky to her house that night. She stated that it was Hollyer who gave the first punch and not Cavanagh. When things had quietened down Ruby said she told Innes and Cavanagh to take Hollyer out into the yard. They had done her bidding but she saw Innes strike the helpless man in the face and then saw Cavanagh repeatedly attacking him. Wright said she did not know if Cavanagh was using his fists or a knife. Blood was found on Wright's and Cavanagh's clothing but none was found on Innes. After all the evidence had been heard the jury returned a verdict of not guilty on James Innes and he was discharged. They found Cavanagh guilty of wilful murder and the death sentence was pronounced.

Cavanagh was granted an appeal to have the charge reduced to that of manslaughter which did not carry the death penalty. The appeal was heard on 3 December before Justices Darling, Sankey and Avory. The defence pointed out that Cavanagh did not have a good reputation in Newcastle and it was probable that most of the jury knew of his character which may have swayed their verdict. Also nobody could possibly believe that the five seamen were not drunk and had not contributed to the violence. Cavanagh and Innes had been insulted and were only standing up for their honour. It was also suggested that the penknife used was so small and Cavanagh so drunk he may not have realised it was in his hand. The defence asked if Innes could be called to give evidence at the appeal. Their Lordships pointed out that Innes had not wanted to give evidence at the trial so they would not hear him now. There was no evidence to support the charge being reduced because of provocation and the appeal was dismissed. A reprieve was also denied by the Home Secretary.

At 8 am on Tuesday, 18 December Cavanagh was escorted to the scaffold within Newcastle Gaol. It was said that he walked to his doom with firm steps. Cavanagh was hanged by Thomas Pierrepoint assisted by Robert Baxter.

CHAPTER 28

I Love You to Death
1919

Not once did he show any remorse ...

In early July, 1919, at the age of twenty-five, Rebecca Jane Quinn took up employment as housekeeper at 15 West Row in Bebside for two miners, Elijah Smith and his brother. She had previously served for four years in the WAAC. Rebecca perhaps had need of a job more than most young women as she had a young child who stayed with her parents at 94 New Row, New Delavel. Around about the time she moved to Bebside, Rebecca began courting Ernest Bernard Scott who was a twenty-eight-year-old ex naval stoker now employed as a miner. The couple had kept company for about three weeks when Scott began pushing for marriage. Rebecca, quite rightly, felt it was too soon and, feeling the relationship was becoming stifling, ended it.

Margaret Davison lived at 69 West Row and had become firm friends with Rebecca. On Monday, 11 August, Scott came to Margaret's door and asked her to convey a message to Rebecca telling her that her child had had

Rebecca Jane Quinn, murdered by Ernest Scott in 1919. Author's collection an accident. Margaret delivered the message accordingly and returned home. Rebecca was, understandably, very upset and, a short while later, called for Margaret asking her to go with her to see her child. After making arrangements for someone to look after her children, Margaret set off with Rebecca towards New Delaval, a distance of just over a mile. The two women had not walked far when they saw Scott. He came towards them and asked what had taken them so long. The women explained they had spent some little time seeing Margaret's children were looked after. As they continued walking Margaret asked Scott if he was going back to work. Scott replied that he was not and his employers knew he was on this errand. Scott then put his arms around Rebecca as if to kiss her so Margaret looked away. No more than a few seconds passed when Margaret looked back to see her friend stumble and fall. She could hardly believe what she was seeing and screamed as she realised Rebecca's clothes were covered in blood.

William Wilkinson was heading towards the railway station and had seen two women and a man walking along the path. He saw one of the women fall and heard the other scream so ran to them to offer assistance. From the corner of his eye he saw the man run off towards Bebside. Wilkinson knelt down beside the woman lying on the ground. On turning her over he saw two severe wounds to her throat and by her shallow breathing he knew nothing could be done to help her. Within minutes Rebecca was dead.

A search for Scott was immediately launched. PC Armstrong from Cowpen

A razor similar to this would have been used by Ernest Scott to cut Rebecca Quinn's throat. The author

was on his bicycle when he spotted Scott at Kitty Brewster and arrested him. Scott offered no resistance and on the way to Blyth police station said:

> *I've not slept all night. Rebecca has given me up and was with another man last night. That is more than I can stand and if you had not caught me I intended to finish myself in the river.*

Scott was charged with Rebecca's murder and after a number of court appearances was sent to take his trial at Newcastle on 5 November before Justice Lawrence.

Dr T Gallagher had attended the scene of the crime shortly after Rebecca's death. According to his medical evidence her death had been caused by two savage blows inflicted by a razor that had severed her windpipe and cut through to the bone of her neck.

Scott refused any sort of defence and when asked if he wanted to give evidence he declined. He stated that he was guilty of taking Rebecca's life but not guilty of murder. A letter was produced addressed to Elijah Smith that had been left at

The Newcastle Assizes in 2003. It was here that Ernest Scott stood trial for the murder of Rebecca Jane Quinn in 1919. The author

Margaret Davison's house on the morning he had called with the so-called message for Rebecca:

Just a few lines to let you know I cannot part with my love so easily. I am doing this for the love of her. There is nothing wrong with the child, but I cannot part from Becky. In death we will be happy, the same as the nights we passed together. God forgive this rash act, but it is for the best. Here is my goodbye and Becky's. Love to all we left. Only forgive me Mr Smith. Ernest Scott Rebecca Quinn

The letter, the witness statements and the hard evidence all pointed to a premeditated and calculated murder. Rebecca's child had come to no misfortune. This had been a lie to lure Rebecca out into the fields. The jury took only twenty minutes to return a verdict of guilty and the entire proceedings took just a little over an hour. Not only had he murdered a girl he was supposed to love, he had deprived a child of its mother. Perhaps if Scott had accepted advice as to his defence he may have used a plea of insanity but it seems he wanted to die in the mistaken notion that he would then be with the girl he loved forever. Scott made no attempt to appeal and remained calm and composed while waiting for the day of reckoning. Not once did he show any remorse for what he had done. He even managed to keep a sense of humour as he wrote in a letter to a friend:

This is a good Government we have now; do you not see my new suit? See how low it is around the neck! You know what this fashion is for.

Ernest Scott's wish for death was fulfilled when he was hanged at Newcastle at 8am on Wednesday, 26 November by John Ellis assisted by Edward Taylor.

CHAPTER 29

The Jealous Serviceman
1919

... Quinn walked up to his wife ... and cut her throat with a razor.

Ambrose Quinn had worked as a labourer for Armstrong, Whitworth and Co at Elswick up until 1917 when he joined the Royal Air Force. His wife of five years, Elizabeth Ann, was left to look after their two small children, one two and one four, and keep house for her widowed father at 63 Hawes Street. Quinn came home on leave in June 1919 after which he was to be sent to India. It was not a happy homecoming as the couple did not see eye to eye on Elizabeth's social life. At twenty-eight Quinn was extremely jealous of his twenty-five-year-old wife. She liked to go out, especially to the pictures, but her husband objected to her doing so. On 19 July the couple had a terrible row because Elizabeth wanted to go to a dance being held that night. Her husband eventually backed down and she attended the dance. Quinn was probably still angry over his wife not doing as he wished and perhaps spoke to someone about the situation. This would have given a gossip an opening and someone certainly fuelled Quinn's anger that same night. Quinn heard that his wife had attended a wedding and later been escorted home by two men. One of the men, Joseph Shepherd, had gone as far as Scotswood Road leaving the other man to walk Elizabeth to her father's house. Quinn was told that this second man and Elizabeth had stopped in a passageway and made love. When Quinn asked his wife if the story was true she was adamant in her denial. Quinn then spoke to Shepherd who agreed that he had left Elizabeth in the company of a man but refused to divulge his name. Elizabeth said she did not know the man's name and asked Shepherd to tell her husband who he was as she had done nothing wrong. Eventually Shepherd told Quinn who the man was. Things went downhill after that with Quinn calling Elizabeth names and in early August he left her. He threatened to take the children from her as she was an unfit mother. Over the next few days Quinn returned again and again to Hawes Street accusing his wife of adultery and uttering threats against her. On Saturday, 9 August, Quinn went out drinking and returned to the house at 10.30pm. His wife was standing outside talking with a group of female neighbours. With no warning Quinn walked up to his wife, put his arms around her from behind and cut her throat with a razor. The screams of one of the women that were present brought a man running from his house a few doors away. The mortally wounded Elizabeth staggered into the man's arms soaking his shirt with blood before falling heavily to the pavement. Quinn was standing on the opposite side of the street but ran off towards Scotswood Road when he saw the man appear.

Elizabeth Ann Quinn, murdered by her husband in 1919 because he thought she was seeing another man. Author's collection

Ambrose Quinn, who was executed for the murder of his wife in 1919. Author's collection

A few minutes later Quinn presented himself at Scotswood Road police station and said a woman had been killed at Hawes Street. Superintendent Potts noticed blood on the man's hands and coat so detained him while he went to investigate. On finding Elizabeth dead Quinn was charged with her murder. He did not seem to understand the charge and so it was repeated. Quinn told the police that he did not mean to kill his wife.

Quinn's trial was held on 6 November at Newcastle before Justice Lawrence. Witness after witness came forward to testify that they had seen Quinn cut his wife's throat. Quinn had been staying at his sister's house and he had taken the razor from there. Thomas Ridley, Elizabeth's father, testified that Quinn was blinded by jealousy and had hit his wife and made threats against her life on numerous occasions. Quinn had gone to the police and told Superintendent Potts that his wife was committing adultery so he wanted to have his separation payments stopped. Potts told him that the police had no

Hawes Street, near Scotswood Road, where Elizabeth Quinn lived with her family. The cross marks the spot where Elizabeth fell. Author's collection

jurisdiction over those matters but advised him on the course of action he would have to take. Quinn also said that his wife was neglecting their children. Potts followed that complaint up and called at Hawes Street but found the children to be well cared for so no action was taken.

A close-up view of number 63 Hawes Street. Author's collection

Elizabeth Quinn's funeral as her body was taken to be interred at Elswick Cemetery. Newcastle Illustrated Chronicle

Quinn's defence was that he only meant to frighten Elizabeth and had no intention of killing her. He maintained that he had no memory of the event at all. The jury was out for only a matter of minutes before finding Quinn guilty of Elizabeth's murder. They did, however, put forward a strong recommendation for mercy. Mercy was denied and Quinn was hanged in Newcastle Gaol at 9.15am on Wednesday, 26 November by John Ellis assisted by Robert Baxter.

These two last cases have similarities which are rather strange. Quinn was the surname of one of the perpetrators and both of the victims. The ages of the two couples were the same. The motive, method and weapon were identical. Both crimes took place in August within two days of one another which meant the trials were held at the same Assizes before the same judge. Both men were hanged on the same gallows on the same morning. These were the last executions to take place at Newcastle. Following 1919, felons who were sentenced to death at Newcastle were executed at Durham.

Acknowledgements

Brian Elliott, Series Editor, for his constructive comments and assistance. The staff at Newcastle Central Library for their quick and efficient service. Hartlepool Reference Library staff who are always courteous and helpful. Jim, my husband, for his usual patience and support.

Sources

An Impartial History of Newcastle upon Tyne, John Baillie, 1801
Local Records of Remarkable Events, John Sykes, Volumes I–II, 1833
Local Records of Remarkable Events, T Fordyce, Volumes III–IV, 1876
The Borderer's Table Book, M A Richardson, Volumes I–VI, 1846
My Experiences as an Executioner, James Berry, 1892
Executioner: Pierrepoint, 1974
The Common Hangman, James Bland, 1984
Hangmen of England, Brian Bailey, 1989
Diary of a Hangman, John Ellis, True Crime Library, 1996
The Encyclopaedia of Executions, John J Eddleston, 2002
The Shadow of the Gallows, Barry Redfern, 2003
Northern Daily Mail, July 1910
Northern Daily Mail, August & November, 1919
Newcastle Illustrated Chronicle, 1875, 1886, 1910, 1913, 1919
Newcastle Courant, 1947
South Durham Herald (various dates)

Index